Spring

CONFIDENT KNITTING

A third year of techniques

Summer

Autumn

Winter

ARNALL-CULLIFORD KNITWEAR

CONFIDENT KNITTING

Introduction

JIM AND JEN ARNALL-CULLIFORD

"Knit on, with confidence and hope, through all crises."
Elizabeth Zimmermann,
The Opinionated Knitter, 1910–1999

This quote is one you may well have heard again and again, but it is apt for our times. The soothing, repetitive action of knitting has been cathartic for so many over the past year or so, be they knitters of long standing, new knitters, or those who have returned to knitting. Furthermore, the act of giving a gift of a knitted item has been a way of expressing love and maintaining a connection when we have been kept apart.

For many of us, adapting, or learning new skills, has become a necessity, but we have always believed that there is joy to be derived from mastering new things. The more you learn, the more confident you can be in your ability to learn more.

This book is aimed at increasing your confidence not only in your knitting, but also in your potential as a learner. While we cannot guarantee that you won't make mistakes and have to start again, we firmly believe that each failure can only lead to greater pleasure once you crack the problem. In this way, confidence, resilience and self-belief will grow.

In planning *Confident Knitting*, we drew heavily on our past as chemists, and as teachers. Just as the chemical elements are the building blocks of all matter around us, so the techniques covered in *Confident Knitting* are the building blocks of projects this year and into the future.

It has always been part of our ethos that learning is best as a social activity. We hope that as you work your way through the tutorials and projects in *Confident Knitting* you will share your successes and struggles with our growing community on The Knitalong Hub. Previous experience has shown us that, whatever you are finding hard, someone, somewhere in the world will have a word of advice or encouragement to set you back on the right track.

Casting on is definitely an act of hope; hope that the ball of yarn will be transformed into an object that will be worn and loved for years. That hope often turns into joy, both in the finished item and in the process of creation.

With our stepwise photo tutorials and online videos, you can cast on with confidence and hope, and learn something new whatever the world throws at you.

CONFIDENT KNITTING

Foreword

KAY GARDINER & ANN SHAYNE

We don't know much about knitting.

Which is what we love about knitting.

Despite the fact that we have been knitters for a while now, we constantly find ourselves saying things like "What *are* Vikkel braids, anyway?" and "This German twisted cast on for ribbing? I have no idea."

The never-ending discovery of new cool techniques is why knitting continues to be utterly fascinating to us. It never gets old, the experimentation and trying out and exploring.

And when our fearless guide is Jen Arnall-Culliford, we feel so certain – so safe – in her hands. Maybe it's the format that she has created to teach us, combining a beautiful pattern by a top designer with a specific technique to explore within that project. Along the way, each technique comes alive in Jen's video tutorials that show us – in the clearest possible way – what's going on. The book captures it all in an easy-to-reference volume, so that we're able to check back in at any time.

It's all so smart and tidy. It gives us confidence that we can handle whatever manoeuvre Jen is introducing to us.

The first two books in this series, *A Year of Techniques* and *Boost Your Knitting*, provide dozens of techniques. Now, with *Confident Knitting*, Jen takes us to new heights of cleverness.

Have a look at what's coming your way in the pages ahead:

- ❖ Folded hem
- ❖ Excellent blocking
- ❖ Catching floats
- ❖ Embroidering your knitting
- ❖ Vikkel braids
- ❖ Reversible cables
- ❖ Garter stitch short-row heel
- ❖ Mosaic knitting
- ❖ Modular knitting
- ❖ German twisted cast on for ribbing
- ❖ Grab stitches
- ❖ i-Cord cast off

We know only the rudiments of some of these concepts, and absolutely nothing about most of them. And that's what's so exciting to us. Even if we think we have the hang of catching floats, Jen gives us tips and tricks to make our work even better. She is the opposite of a know-it-all. She just really does seem to know it all.

As we have learned from the earlier books in this series, once we sit down and try out these techniques, we are going to become just a little bit more skilled at this knitting thing.

It helps that the format of this series allows for easy reference. This book will be waiting for you anytime, and Jen's superb video tutorials will be ever ready to watch.

We've long said that this series is as close as we can get to having one-on-one lessons with Jen. In a world where knitters are spread across the globe, *Confident Knitting* is a joyous way to spend time with this superb teacher.

She makes us feel so certain of success. Confident, actually.

Kay Gardiner and Ann Shayne
Co-founders, Modern Daily Knitting
www.ModernDailyKnitting.com

CONFIDENT KNITTING

Contents

Spring

March

TECHNIQUE	**Folded Hem**
PROJECT	**Flux Hand Warmers**
DESIGNER	**Martina Behm**

April

TECHNIQUE	**Excellent Blocking**
PROJECT	**Evolve Cowl**
DESIGNER	**Hunter Hammersen**

May

TECHNIQUE	**Catching Floats**
PROJECT	**Variance Hat**
DESIGNER	**Janette Budge**

TECHNIQUE
FOLDED HEM

Some techniques in knitting really speak to me. I'm talking about the sort of technique that has me reaching for needles and looking for places I can use it within minutes of learning of its existence. When I first learnt to work a folded hem, that was precisely my reaction. It is so elegant! It adds the sort of finish to a project that will make non-knitters question whether the item you are wearing was really made by you. And the best part? A folded hem isn't particularly difficult to do.

Folded hems have lots of uses. Our project, Martina Behm's Flux Hand Warmers, uses one at the cuff. You can equally use it as a cuff on socks or sleeves, or the hem of a sweater, or perhaps you will use it for the brim of a hat? You will find yourself looking at projects and wanting to experiment!

While it is entirely possible to cast on normally, knit a hem, fold it up and sew the edge down, there's something unbelievably satisfying about working seamlessly with your live stitches. It takes both the process, and the finish, up a notch.

This tutorial will walk you through how to work a seamless folded hem, as well as giving a few alternative options for ways to change the look of your edging.

A folded hem consists of three stages:
❖ A provisional cast on, followed by working the inside of the hem on smaller needles.
❖ A turning round, followed by working the outside of the hem with larger needles.
❖ And finally, a joining round completes the hem.

PROVISIONAL CAST ON AND INSIDE HEM

The instructions here will walk you through the crochet provisional cast-on method, but you can use an alternative if you prefer. You then work a number of rounds using a smaller needle size than the one you'll use for the main part of the project. Using a smaller needle for what becomes the inside hem ensures it sits neatly once folded and joined.

TURNING ROUND AND OUTSIDE HEM

Martina's Flux Hand Warmers use a picot turning round where you work a series of yarn over, k2tog pairs to make a pretty picot edge[1]. You can also work a purl round, to give structure to the fold[2]. Or of course you can simply knit the turning round for a smooth curved edge to the hem[3].

Next, switch to larger needles and work the same number of rounds as you worked for the inside of the hem.

JOINING ROUND

The joining round is the meat of the folded hem. To work this round, you unzip your provisional cast-on edge (if you used a method that requires unzipping), and then you work around the stitches, knitting together one of your live stitches with one of the stitches from the cast-on edge. This makes an exceptionally neat join for your hem.

The following photo tutorials use double-pointed needles. The joining round works in just the same way if you use circular needles, as demonstrated in our online video tutorial (**www. acknitwear.co.uk/confident-knitting**).

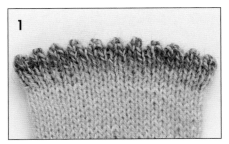

Picot edge: *Yo, k2tog; rep from * to end.

Purl edge: Purl to end.

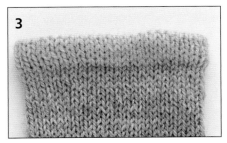

Plain edge: Knit to end.

CROCHET PROVISIONAL CAST-ON METHOD

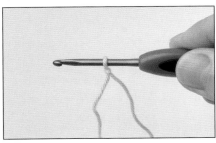

1 Make a slip knot in your waste yarn and place it on your crochet hook.

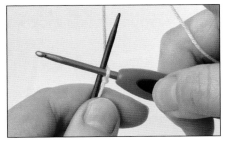

2 Hold the crochet hook over your knitting needle and pass the waste yarn under the needle.

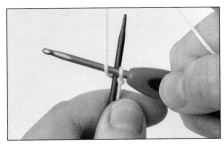

3 Wrap the waste yarn over the hook.

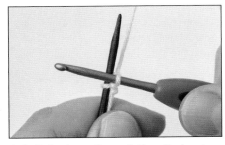

4 Pull the loop through the slip knot. You now have one stitch on your knitting needle.

March

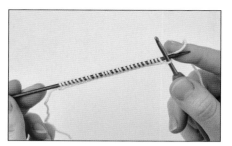

5 Repeat steps 2–4 until you have sufficient stitches on your needle.

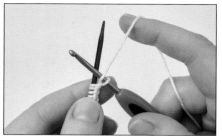

6 Wrap the waste yarn around the hook only, and pull the loop through the stitch on the hook. This creates a chain stitch.

7 Work four or five more chain stitches as in step 6.

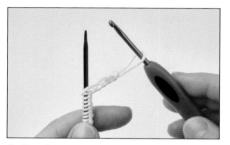

8 Cut the yarn and pull it through the final stitch. This short chain tells you which end to unzip later.

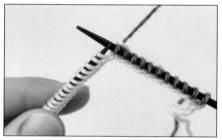

9 Change to main yarn and work as indicated in your pattern.

Knit with smaller needles to create the inside hem. Work your desired turning round, then knit the outside of your hem with larger needles. You are now ready to unzip your cast-on edge and work the joining round.

UNZIPPING YOUR CROCHET PROVISIONAL CAST ON

1 Find the end of the free crochet chain, and pull the waste yarn through the final loop to unravel it.

2 Once the final stitch is free (you may need to pull it through once more to free it), you can gently pull on the end and the chain will unravel.

3 Have your knitting needle ready (it may be easier if it is a smaller needle than the one with which you cast on) and pick up the first stitch revealed in the main yarn.

4 As you gently pull out the waste yarn, pick up the stitches revealed. If you are worried about dropping a stitch, you can pick up the stitch before you pull the waste yarn out.

5 Check that you have the correct number of stitches on your needles. If necessary, pick up an extra stitch from the start of the round.

JOINING ROUND

1 Fold the fabric so that the right side is outermost, and your live needles are parallel with the needles holding the cast-on stitches. The live stitches should be in front of the cast-on stitches. You will now knit together the live and cast-on stitches.

2 Insert your right needle tip into the first live stitch on the front needle, and then through the first cast-on stitch on the rear needle.

3 Knit these stitches together. Steps 4–7 will now show that process in detail.

4 Insert the right needle tip through the first stitch on both front and rear needles.

5 Wrap the main yarn around the right needle tip.

6 Pull the yarn through both stitches.

March

7 Slip both stitches off their respective needles.

8 Repeat steps 4–7 until all live stitches have been joined to cast-on stitches.

This completes your folded hem.

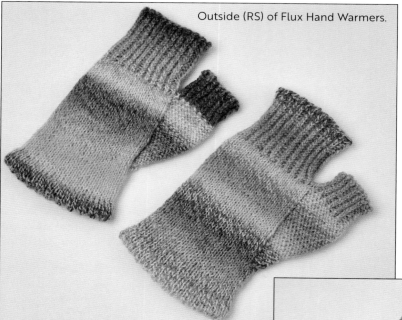

Outside (RS) of Flux Hand Warmers.

I hope you will enjoy this elegant edging, and find uses for it on lots of new projects. What could be better for practising a new skill than a project that requires that skill twice? Martina's pretty Flux Hand Warmers use a folded hem at each cuff and you can choose from three hem options.

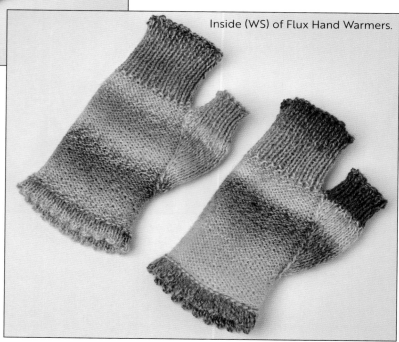

Inside (WS) of Flux Hand Warmers.

PROJECT
FLUX HAND WARMERS

by Martina Behm

Use the folded hem technique to knit these fun, colourful hand warmers.

March

SIZE
Small (Medium, Large, XL)
To fit hand circumference above thumb: 16 (18, 20, 22) cm
[6¼ (7, 7¾, 8¾) in]
Actual wrist circumference: 12.5 (14.5, 16.5, 18.5) cm
[5 (5¾, 6½, 7¼) in]
Actual hand circumference above thumb (rib, unstretched):
10.5 (12, 14, 15.5) cm [4¼ (4¾, 5½, 6) in]
Length: 15.5 (16.5, 18, 19.5) cm [6 (6½, 7, 7½) in]
Shown in size Medium on hand circumference 18cm [7in].

YARN
Schoppel Wolle Zauberball Crazy (4ply/fingering weight;
75% superwash wool, 25% biodegradable nylon; 420m per
100g ball)
Garden Party / Gartenparty 2355; 1 x 100g ball in all sizes
Approximate yardages
100 (120, 150, 180) m [110 (130, 160, 200) yds]

NEEDLES AND NOTIONS
1 set 2.5mm [US 1.5] circular needle, 80cm [32in] long, or
double-pointed needles, or one size smaller than size needed
to match tension, or your preferred needles for working small
circumferences in the round
1 set 2.75mm [US 2] circular needle, 80cm [32in] long, or
double-pointed needles, or size to match tension, or your
preferred needles for working small circumferences in the
round

A small quantity of smooth waste yarn of approximately 4ply
weight
2-3mm crochet hook
Spare double-pointed needle or cable needle
Stitch markers, Tapestry needle

TENSION
30 sts and 42 rounds to 10cm [4in] over stocking stitch
worked in the round, using larger needles, after washing and
blocking
36 sts and 40 rounds to 10cm [4in] over twisted rib worked in
the round, using larger needles, after washing and blocking

ABBREVIATIONS
LLIP   left lifted increase; lift the left leg of the stitch 2
rows below the stitch on your right needle onto the
left needle tip and purl this loop through the back (1
stitch increased)
RLIP   right lifted increase; lift the right leg of the stitch
below the next stitch on the left needle onto the
left needle tip and purl this loop (1 stitch increased)
A full list of abbreviations can be found on page 112.

SPECIAL TECHNIQUES
Photo tutorials for the following techniques can be found
within this book:
Crochet provisional cast-on method (page 9)
Folded hem (pages 9-12)

The following video tutorials can be found on our website at
www.acknitwear.co.uk/confident-knitting
Folded hem
Stretchy cast-off method

PATTERN NOTES
These hand warmers start with a crochet provisional cast
on, and the inside edge of the folded hem is worked with
smaller needles. A turning round with yarn over holes is
worked to form the picot edge (a knit or purl round may be
chosen instead), before larger needles are used to work the
outside edge of the folded hem. A joining round completes
the folded hem before the wrist is knitted in stocking stitch.
A thumb gusset uses purl stitches to give a textural contrast
to the hand and then the thumb stitches are left on a holder
before the hand is completed in twisted ribbing. Finally, the
thumb stitches are worked in twisted rib to complete the
hand warmer.

The pattern is provided in four sizes, but if you wish to make
further adjustments it will be straightforward to add or
remove an even number of stitches to give a smaller or larger
hand circumference. You can also very easily add length by
changing either the plain rounds worked at the wrist, or the
rib rounds worked at the hand, or both.

HAND WARMERS
Make 2 alike.

1 CAST ON AND WORK PICOT EDGING
Using the crochet provisional cast-on method (see page 9) and waste yarn, cast on 38 (44, 50, 56) sts.

Using the main yarn and smaller needles, knit across all stitches.

Join to work in the round, being careful not to twist. Pm for start of round.

Knit 5 (5, 7, 7) rounds.

Turning round: *Yo, k2tog; rep from * to end of round.
This turning round creates the picot effect, alternatively a plain knit or purl round may be used (see examples on page 9).

Change to larger needles.
Knit 6 (6, 8, 8) rounds.

Unzip the crochet provisional cast-on edge (see page 10) and return the sts to the smaller needles.

Joining round: Hold the tips of the two sets of needles together so that the fabric forms a tube, with smooth knit sts outermost. The cast-on edge sts (smaller needles) will be behind the live sts (larger needles). Use the larger needle to knit together the first stitch on front and rear needles. Repeat until all cast-on edge sts have been joined to the live sts and the round is complete. This is shown in full in the photo tutorial on pages 11–12.

2 WORK WRIST AND THUMB GUSSET
Knit 12 (12, 14, 14) rounds.

Round 1: Place next st on a spare DPN or cable needle and hold it in front of your knitting, knit next stitch through the back loop, then knit the stitch from the DPN through the back loop, knit to end.
Round 2 (inc): K1 tbl, lift bar between sts and knit into it tbl, k1 tbl, knit to end. *1 st inc; 39 (45, 51, 57) sts.*
Round 3: K1 tbl, p1, k1 tbl, knit to end.
Round 4 (inc): K1 tbl, p1, LLIP, k1 tbl, knit to end. *1 st inc; 40 (46, 52, 58) sts.*
Round 5 (inc): K1 tbl, RLIP, p2, k1 tbl, knit to end. *1 st inc; 41 (47, 53, 59) sts.*
Round 6: K1 tbl, p3, k1 tbl, knit to end.
Round 7 (inc): K1 tbl, RLIP, p3, LLIP, k1 tbl, knit to end. *2 sts inc; 43 (49, 55, 61) sts.*
Round 8: K1 tbl, purl all purl stitches, k1 tbl, knit to end.
Round 9 (inc): K1 tbl, RLIP, purl all purl stitches, LLIP, k1 tbl, knit to end. *2 sts inc.*

Rep rounds 8 and 9 a further 8 (10, 10, 12) times. *18 (22, 22, 26) sts inc; 61 (71, 77, 87) sts.*

You should now have 23 (27, 27, 31) purl sts between the twisted st columns. These purl sts will become the thumb.

3 HAND RIBBING
Round 1 (set aside thumb): K1 tbl, slip the next 23 (27, 27, 31) purl sts to waste yarn, p1, *k1 tbl, p1; rep from * to end. *38 (44, 50, 56) sts remain.*

Round 2: *K1 tbl, p1; rep from * to end.
Last round sets twisted rib pattern. Work a further 18 (18, 20, 22) rounds in twisted rib as set.

Cast off all sts with a stretchy method, or using larger needles.

4 THUMB
Return the 23 (27, 27, 31) thumb sts to larger needles. Pick up and knit 3 sts at the base of the thumb to close any gap that might form there, now work across the 23 (27, 27, 31) thumb sts as follows: *k1 tbl, p1; rep from * to last st, k1 tbl. *26 (30, 30, 34) sts.*

Pm for start of round.

Round 1 (dec): K2tog, p1, *k1 tbl, p1; rep from * to last 3 sts, k1 tbl, p2tog. *2 sts dec; 24 (28, 28, 32) sts remain.*
Round 2: *K1 tbl, p1; rep from * to end.
Last round sets twisted rib pattern. Work a further 6 rounds in twisted rib as set.

Cast off all sts with a stretchy method, or using larger needles.

5 FINISHING
Weave in ends. Soak your hand warmers in lukewarm water with wool wash for 20 minutes. Squeeze out excess water. Lay flat to measurements, and allow to dry.

TECHNIQUE
EXCELLENT BLOCKING

At its simplest, blocking is the process of washing and drying your knitted fabric. Almost all knitting will be improved by a simple wash and dry. Add to that a little bit of time spent evening up your stitches, or in the case of lace, stretching them out, and you have a process that can transform your knitting. I often think of blocking as like blow-drying your hair – it's a process that needs to be repeated each time you wash the item, and the more care you take over the styling as it dries, the better the result!

For this month's technique, we have two options for blocking a cowl. Lace cowls are among the trickier items to block, as ideally you will dry them in a way that stretches out the lace, but doesn't create any folds in the fabric.

Unblocked:
This cowl is fresh off the needles, and is different to its intended shape. The bottom edge is curling, and the lace pattern is indistinct.

Blocked:
The cowl now has its intended graceful shape, with the lace pattern opened out. The sinuous lines of the stitch pattern are much more visible. The bottom edge has a pretty scalloped shape and lies flat.

April

BLOCKING A COWL

3 Once your cowl is damp, it is time to fuss with it, to get the most out of your stitch pattern! You can simply lay your cowl flat on a towel and leave it to dry, but this will leave creases in the fabric, so it is worth returning and moving the cowl every hour or so to avoid this.

1 The first stage in the blocking process is to soak your cowl in lukewarm water with a little wool wash for around 20 minutes. This gives time for the water to thoroughly soak into the fibres. If required, rinse out the wool wash.

2 Once the cowl is fully soaked, remove it from the water and squeeze (but don't wring) to remove the excess water. You can roll the wet cowl up in a towel to remove the majority of the water, if desired.

5 If space is at a premium, you can hang a cowl to dry over a suitable cylinder shape (right). Here I've used the same plumbers' pipe insulation, but again, any number of similarly shaped household objects would also work. You may wish to move the cowl as it dries, to ensure that all of the cowl is equally stretched (the section over the foam stretches more than that at the bottom). This is a simple, but effective method.

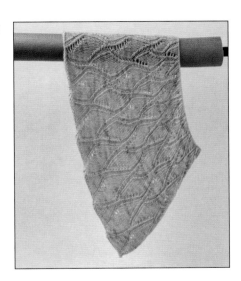

4 To avoid forming creases at the folded edge, you can use a pair of suitable cylindrical objects at the sides of your cowl while it dries. Here I have used a length of plumbers' pipe insulation at each edge, and this allows the cowl to dry without forming a crease. You could also use rolls of kitchen towels (an unopened pack), plastic tubing, or any other similar object that won't mind getting a bit damp.

BLOCKING A COWL USING WIRES AND PINS

For maximum stretch and a perfect result every time, you can use a combination of flexible blocking wires and pins, along with some household objects to block your cowl.

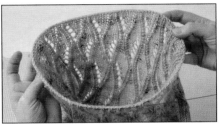

1 Work steps 1 and 2 from the tutorial above on blocking a cowl. Thread a flexible wire around the cast-off edge of your cowl, taking in a stitch or two each time.

2 When you reach the beginning, overlap the first few stitches with the ends of your wire.

3 Gently pull the cast-off edge outwards, ensuring that the ends of the wire remain overlapped. The tension of the wire should ensure that you can open it up fully.

April

4 Use another flexible wire to thread along the cast-on edge. In the chart for the Evolve Cowl, it indicates a good point at which to thread through your wire, to give an attractive scalloped edge to your cowl.

5 If required, you can overlap more than one wire in order to complete the circumference of the cast-on edge.

6 Thread two straight knitting needles, chopsticks or similar alternative, across the top of the cowl at the cast-off edge, to form a cross shape.

7 Sit the crossed needles on top of a suitable cylinder. I've used a roll of kitchen towels here, but a wide-necked drinks bottle or other tall cylinder is perfect.

8 If your first item isn't tall enough, add further objects underneath. We have used a coffee pot, but you can improvise with what you have to hand!

9 You want your cowl to be lifted up so that the cast-on edge just sits on the blocking surface. My kitchen roll and coffee pot combination is perfect!

10 Now pin out the points where you threaded the wires through the cast-on edge, so that the cowl is fully stretched. Start by pinning out the opposite edges, and then divide each section in half. Your cowl should now be well stretched out.

11 Make final adjustments by checking that each point is pinned out evenly.

Blocking is such a satisfying process. Hunter's Evolve Cowl is the perfect project on which to develop your blocking skills.

12 If your cast-off edge is sagging a little, you can add extra knitting needles (or whatever you are using to suspend the cowl) to keep it level. Once dry, you can unpin and unthread the wires and enjoy your perfectly blocked cowl.

PROJECT
EVOLVE COWL

by Hunter Hammersen

Excellent blocking allows the sinuous lines and eyelets of this elegant cowl to sing.

April

SIZE

Small (Medium, Large, XL)
Cowl circumference at shoulders: 85.5 (93.5, 101, 109) cm [33¾ (36¾, 39¾, 42¾) in]
Cowl circumference at neck (short version): 49 (53.5, 58, 62) cm [19¼ (21, 22¾, 24½) in]
Cowl circumference at neck (long version): 43 (46.5, 50.5, 54.5) cm [16¾ (18¼, 20, 21½) in]
Depth (short version): 36cm [14¼in]
Depth (long version): 39cm [15½in]
Shown in size XL, short version, on shoulder circumference 99cm [39in].

YARN

Dusty Dimples Dusty Worsted (DK weight; 100% superwash merino; 230m per 115g skein)
Rosehall; 2 x 115g skeins in all sizes
Alternative yarn suggestion: Fyberspates Vivacious DK (DK weight; 100% superwash merino; 230m per 115g skein)
Shoreline (825); 2 x 115g skeins in all sizes
Approximate yardages
Short version: 255 (280, 300, 325) m [280 (305, 330, 355) yds]
Long version: 265 (290, 315, 340) m [290 (320, 345, 370) yds]

NEEDLES AND NOTIONS

1 set 4.5mm [US 7] circular needles, 60cm [24in] long, or size to match tension, or your preferred needles for working medium circumferences in the round
1 set 4.5mm [US 7] circular needles, 40cm [16in] long, or size to match tension, or your preferred needles for working medium circumferences in the round
Stitch marker
Tapestry needle
Blocking kit: flexible wires and rust-proof pins, or two waterproof cylindrical objects, e.g. plumbers' pipe insulation

TENSION

18 sts and 25 rounds to 10cm [4in] over lace pattern worked in the round, relaxed after washing and blocking
It is vital to match the washed and firmly blocked tension here, or you may run short of yarn.

ABBREVIATIONS

RLTD   right-leaning twisted knit decrease; Slip next stitch purlwise, remount the next stitch by rotating it 180° clockwise, return slipped stitch to left needle, knit these two stitches together (1 stitch decreased)
A full list of abbreviations can be found on page 112.

SPECIAL TECHNIQUES

Photo tutorials for the following techniques can be found within this book:
Excellent blocking (pages 17–18)

The following video tutorials can be found on our website at
www.acknitwear.co.uk/confident-knitting
Blocking a cowl
Blocking a cowl using wires and pins

PATTERN NOTES

This cowl is worked in the round, starting at the widest point and then getting narrower as you work upwards. The lace pattern cleverly incorporates the shaping to give a flowing evolution of the stitch pattern.

As the recommended yarn is hand-dyed, we would suggest alternating skeins of yarn in single-round stripes. Once your first skein is nearly finished, stop knitting with it at the start of the round marker, leaving a tail to weave in later. Then continue with one skein only. This will blend in any small differences between the two skeins.

The pattern is provided in four sizes, but if you wish to make further adjustments they can be made as follows:
To adjust the circumference you can add or remove a multiple of 14 stitches to give a wider or narrower shoulder circumference. The cowl can also be made shorter by ending at round 80 rather than rounds 90 or 98, thereby omitting the final iteration(s) of the pattern. It is also possible to adjust both circumference and height by working at a different gauge by changing your needle size or the weight of yarn chosen, but you will need to be sure that you are getting a fabric that you like and that you have sufficient yarn for this approach.

Instructions are provided in both written and charted forms.

CHART NOTES

The cowl is worked in the round, so all chart rows are read from right to left.

COWL

1 CAST ON AND WORK LACE – CHARTED INSTRUCTIONS

Using your favourite stretchy cast-on method (shown here with the long-tail cast on), cast on 154 (168, 182, 196) sts. Join to work in the round, being careful not to twist. Pm for start of round.

Round 1: Reading from right to left, work across row 1 of chart A 11 (12, 13, 14) times. Last round sets chart A pattern. Continue to work from chart A, decreasing as indicated, until chart row 52 is complete. *22 (24, 26, 28) sts dec; 132 (144, 156, 168) sts remain.*

Round 53: Reading from right to left, work across row 53 of chart B 11 (12, 13, 14) times. Last round sets chart B pattern. Continue to work from chart B, decreasing as indicated and changing to a shorter needle if required, until chart row 90 is complete. *44 (48, 52, 56) sts dec; 88 (96, 104, 112) sts remain.*

Short version
Move to step 3.

Long version
Work chart rows 91–98. *11 (12, 13, 14) sts dec; 77 (84, 91, 98) sts remain.*
Move to step 3.

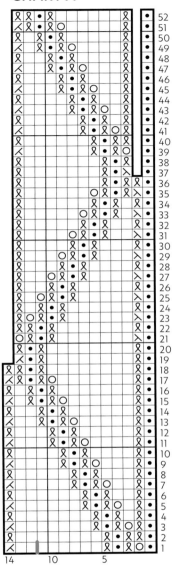

CHART A

CHART B

KEY

☐	Knit
•	Purl
⍉	K1 tbl
⤬	K2tog tbl
⍂	Right-leaning twisted knit decrease; Slip 1 purlwise, rotate next stitch 180° clockwise return slipped st to left needle, k2tog
O	Yarn over
❙	Suggested position to thread wires through when blocking

2 CAST ON AND WORK LACE – WRITTEN INSTRUCTIONS
Using your favourite stretchy cast-on method (shown here with the long-tail cast on), cast on 154 (168, 182, 196) sts. Join to work in the round, being careful not to twist. Pm for start of round.

Round 1: *P1, yo, k1 tbl, p1, k1 tbl, k8, RLTD; rep from * to end.

Round 2: *P1, [k1 tbl] twice, p1, k1 tbl, k8, k1 tbl; rep from * to end.

Round 3: *P1, k1 tbl, yo, k1 tbl, p1, k1 tbl, k7, RLTD; rep from * to end.

Round 4: *P1, k1 tbl, k1, k1 tbl, p1, k1 tbl, k7, k1 tbl; rep from * to end.

Round 5: *P1, k1 tbl, k1, yo, k1 tbl, p1, k1 tbl, k6, RLTD; rep from * to end.

Round 6: *P1, k1 tbl, k2, k1 tbl, p1, k1 tbl, k6, k1 tbl; rep from * to end.

Round 7: *P1, k1 tbl, k2, yo, k1 tbl, p1, k1 tbl, k5, RLTD; rep from * to end.

Round 8: *P1, k1 tbl, k3, k1 tbl, p1, k1 tbl, k5, k1 tbl; rep from * to end.

Round 9: *P1, k1 tbl, k3, yo, k1 tbl, p1, k1 tbl, k4, RLTD; rep from * to end.

Round 10: *P1, k1 tbl, k4, k1 tbl, p1, k1 tbl, k4, k1 tbl; rep from * to end.

Round 11: *P1, k1 tbl, k4, yo, k1 tbl, p1, k1 tbl, k3, RLTD; rep from * to end.

Round 12: *P1, k1 tbl, k5, k1 tbl, p1, k1 tbl, k3, k1 tbl; rep from * to end.

Round 13: *P1, k1 tbl, k5, yo, k1 tbl, p1, k1 tbl, k2, RLTD; rep from * to end.

Round 14: *P1, k1 tbl, k6, k1 tbl, p1, k1 tbl, k2, k1 tbl; rep from * to end.

Round 15: *P1, k1 tbl, k6, yo, k1 tbl, p1, k1 tbl, k1, RLTD; rep from * to end.

Round 16: *P1, k1 tbl, k7, k1 tbl, p1, k1 tbl, k1, k1 tbl; rep from * to end.

Round 17: *P1, k1 tbl, k7, yo, k1 tbl, p1, k1 tbl, RLTD; rep from * to end.

Round 18: *P1, k1 tbl, k8, k1 tbl, p1, [k1 tbl] twice; rep from * to end.

Round 19 (dec): *P1, k1 tbl, k8, k1 tbl, p1, RLTD; rep from * to end. *11 (12, 13, 14) sts dec; 143 (156, 169, 182) sts remain.*

Round 20: *P1, k1 tbl, k8, k1 tbl, p1, k1 tbl; rep from * to end.

Round 21: *P1, k2tog tbl, k7, k1 tbl, p1, k1 tbl, yo; rep from * to end.

Round 22: *P1, k1 tbl, k7, k1 tbl, p1, [k1 tbl] twice; rep from * to end.

Round 23: *P1, k2tog tbl, k6, k1 tbl, p1, k1 tbl, yo, k1 tbl; rep from * to end.

Round 24: *P1, k1 tbl, k6, k1 tbl, p1, k1 tbl, k1, k1 tbl; rep from * to end.

Round 25: *P1, k2tog tbl, k5, k1 tbl, p1, k1 tbl, yo, k1, k1 tbl; rep from * to end.

Round 26: *P1, k1 tbl, k5, k1 tbl, p1, k1 tbl, k2, k1 tbl; rep from * to end.

Round 27: *P1, k2tog tbl, k4, k1 tbl, p1, k1 tbl, yo, k2, k1 tbl; rep from * to end.

Round 28: *P1, k1 tbl, k4, k1 tbl, p1, k1 tbl, k3, k1 tbl; rep from * to end.

Round 29: *P1, k2tog tbl, k3, k1 tbl, p1, k1 tbl, yo, k3, k1 tbl; rep from * to end.

Round 30: *P1, k1 tbl, k3, k1 tbl, p1, k1 tbl, k4, k1 tbl; rep from * to end.

Round 31: *P1, k2tog tbl, k2, k1 tbl, p1, k1 tbl, yo, k4, k1 tbl; rep from * to end.

Round 32: *P1, k1 tbl, k2, k1 tbl, p1, k1 tbl, k5, k1 tbl; rep from * to end.

Round 33: *P1, k2tog tbl, k1, k1 tbl, p1, k1 tbl, yo, k5, k1 tbl; rep from * to end.

Round 34: *P1, k1 tbl, k1, k1 tbl, p1, k1 tbl, k6, k1 tbl; rep from * to end.

Round 35: *P1, k2tog tbl, k1 tbl, p1, k1 tbl, yo, k6, k1 tbl; rep from * to end.

Round 36: *P1, [k1 tbl] twice, p1, k1 tbl, k7, k1 tbl; rep from * to end.

Round 37 (dec): *P1, k2tog tbl, p1, k1 tbl, k7, k1 tbl; rep from * to end. *11 (12, 13, 14) sts dec; 132 (144, 156, 168) sts remain.*

Round 38: *[P1, k1 tbl] twice, k7, k1 tbl; rep from * to end.

Round 39: *P1, yo, k1 tbl, p1, k1 tbl, k6, RLTD; rep from * to end.

Round 40: *P1, [k1 tbl] twice, p1, k1 tbl, k6, k1 tbl; rep from * to end.

Round 41: *P1, k1 tbl, yo, k1 tbl, p1, k1 tbl, k5, RLTD; rep from * to end.

Round 42: *P1, k1 tbl, k1, k1 tbl, p1, k1 tbl, k5, k1 tbl; rep from * to end.

Round 43: *P1, k1 tbl, k1, yo, k1 tbl, p1, k1 tbl, k4, RLTD; rep from * to end.

Round 44: *P1, k1 tbl, k2, k1 tbl, p1, k1 tbl, k4, k1 tbl; rep from * to end.

Round 45: *P1, k1 tbl, k2, yo, k1 tbl, p1, k1 tbl, k3, RLTD; rep from * to end.

Round 46: *P1, k1 tbl, k3, k1 tbl, p1, k1 tbl, k3, k1 tbl; rep from * to end.

Round 47: *P1, k1 tbl, k3, yo, k1 tbl, p1, k1 tbl, k2, RLTD; rep from * to end.

Round 48: *P1, k1 tbl, k4, k1 tbl, p1, k1 tbl, k2, k1 tbl; rep from * to end.

Round 49: *P1, k1 tbl, k4, yo, k1 tbl, p1, k1 tbl, k1, RLTD; rep from * to end.

Round 50: *P1, k1 tbl, k5, k1 tbl, p1, k1 tbl, k1, k1 tbl; rep from * to end.

Round 51: *P1, k1 tbl, k5, yo, k1 tbl, p1, k1 tbl, RLTD; rep from * to end.

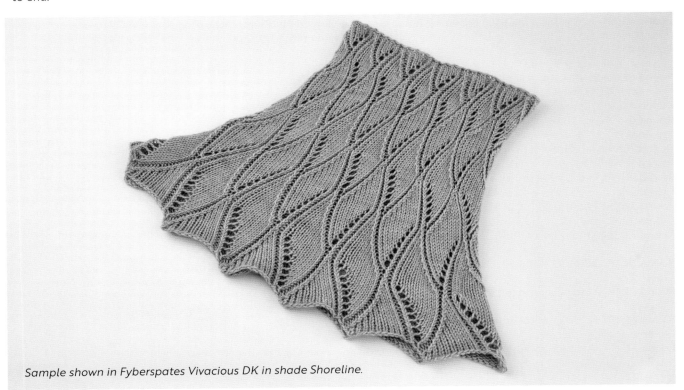

Sample shown in Fyberspates Vivacious DK in shade Shoreline.

April

Round 52: *P1, k1 tbl, k6, k1 tbl, p1, [k1 tbl] twice; rep from * to end.

In the following section, change to a shorter needle if required.

Round 53 (dec): *P1, k1 tbl, k6, k1 tbl, p1, RLTD; rep from * to end. *11 (12, 13, 14) sts dec; 121 (132, 143, 154) sts remain.*
Round 54: *P1, k1 tbl, k6, k1 tbl, p1, k1 tbl; rep from * to end.
Round 55: *P1, k2tog tbl, k5, k1 tbl, p1, k1 tbl, yo; rep from * to end.
Round 56: *P1, k1 tbl, k5, k1 tbl, p1, [k1 tbl] twice; rep from * to end.
Round 57: *P1, k2tog tbl, k4, k1 tbl, p1, k1 tbl, yo, k1 tbl; rep from * to end.
Round 58: *P1, k1 tbl, k4, k1 tbl, p1, k1 tbl, k1, k1 tbl; rep from * to end.
Round 59: *P1, k2tog tbl, k3, k1 tbl, p1, k1 tbl, yo, k1, k1 tbl; rep from * to end.
Round 60: *P1, k1 tbl, k3, k1 tbl, p1, k1 tbl, k2, k1 tbl; rep from * to end.
Round 61: *P1, k2tog tbl, k2, k1 tbl, p1, k1 tbl, yo, k2, k1 tbl; rep from * to end.
Round 62: *P1, k1 tbl, k2, k1 tbl, p1, k1 tbl, k3, k1 tbl; rep from * to end.
Round 63: *P1, k2tog tbl, k1, k1 tbl, p1, k1 tbl, yo, k3, k1 tbl; rep from * to end.
Round 64: *P1, k1 tbl, k1, k1 tbl, p1, k1 tbl, k4, k1 tbl; rep from * to end.
Round 65: *P1, k2tog tbl, k1 tbl, p1, k1 tbl, yo, k4, k1 tbl; rep from * to end.
Round 66: *P1, [k1 tbl] twice, p1, k1 tbl, k5, k1 tbl; rep from * to end.
Round 67 (dec): *P1, k2tog tbl, p1, k1 tbl, k5, k1 tbl; rep from * to end. *11 (12, 13, 14) sts dec; 110 (120, 130, 140) sts remain.*
Round 68: *[P1, k1 tbl] twice, k5, k1 tbl; rep from * to end.
Round 69: *P1, yo, k1 tbl, p1, k1 tbl, k4, RLTD; rep from * to end.
Round 70: *P1, [k1 tbl] twice, p1, k1 tbl, k4, k1 tbl; rep from * to end.
Round 71: *P1, k1 tbl, yo, k1 tbl, p1, k1 tbl, k3, RLTD; rep from * to end.
Round 72: *P1, k1 tbl, k1, k1 tbl, p1, k1 tbl, k3, k1 tbl; rep from * to end.
Round 73: *P1, k1 tbl, k1, yo, k1 tbl, p1, k1 tbl, k2, RLTD; rep from * to end.
Round 74: *P1, k1 tbl, k2, k1 tbl, p1, k1 tbl, k2, k1 tbl; rep from * to end.
Round 75: *P1, k1 tbl, k2, yo, k1 tbl, p1, k1 tbl, k1, RLTD; rep from * to end.
Round 76: *P1, k1 tbl, k3, k1 tbl, p1, k1 tbl, k1, k1 tbl; rep from * to end.
Round 77: *P1, k1 tbl, k3, yo, k1 tbl, p1, k1 tbl, RLTD; rep from * to end.

Round 78: *P1, k1 tbl, k4, k1 tbl, p1, [k1 tbl] twice; rep from * to end.
Round 79 (dec): *P1, k1 tbl, k4, k1 tbl, p1, RLTD; rep from * to end. *11 (12, 13, 14) sts dec; 99 (108, 117, 126) sts remain.*
Round 80: *P1, k1 tbl, k4, k1 tbl, p1, k1 tbl; rep from * to end.
Round 81: *P1, k2tog tbl, k3, k1 tbl, p1, k1tbl, yo; rep from * to end.
Round 82: *P1, k1 tbl, k3, k1 tbl, p1, [k1 tbl] twice; rep from * to end.
Round 83: *P1, k2tog tbl, k2, k1 tbl, p1, k1 tbl, yo, k1 tbl; rep from * to end.
Round 84: *P1, k1 tbl, k2, k1 tbl, p1, k1 tbl, k1, k1 tbl; rep from * to end.
Round 85: *P1, k2tog tbl, k1, k1 tbl, p1, k1 tbl, yo, k1, k1 tbl; rep from * to end.
Round 86: *P1, k1 tbl, k1, k1 tbl, p1, k1 tbl, k2, k1 tbl; rep from * to end.
Round 87: *P1, k2tog tbl, k1 tbl, p1, k1 tbl, yo, k2, k1 tbl; rep from * to end.
Round 88: *P1, [k1 tbl] twice, p1, k1 tbl, k3, k1 tbl; rep from * to end.
Round 89 (dec): *P1, k2tog tbl, p1, k1 tbl, k3, k1 tbl; rep from * to end. *11 (12, 13, 14) sts dec; 88 (96, 104, 112) sts remain.*
Round 90: *[P1, k1 tbl] twice, k3, k1 tbl; rep from * to end.

Short version
Move to step 3.

Long version
Round 91: *P1, yo, k1 tbl, p1, k1 tbl, k2, RLTD; rep from * to end.
Round 92: *P1, [k1 tbl] twice, p1, k1 tbl, k2, k1 tbl; rep from * to end.
Round 93: *P1, k1 tbl, yo, k1 tbl, p1, k1 tbl, k1, RLTD; rep from * to end.
Round 94: *P1, k1 tbl, k1, k1 tbl, p1, k1 tbl, k1, k1 tbl; rep from * to end.
Round 95: *P1, k1 tbl, k1, yo, k1 tbl, p1, k1 tbl, RLTD; rep from * to end.
Round 96: *P1, k1 tbl, k2, k1 tbl, p1, [k1 tbl] twice; rep from * to end.
Round 97 (dec): *P1, k1 tbl, k2, k1 tbl, p1, RLTD; rep from * to end. *11 (12, 13, 14) sts dec; 77 (84, 91, 98) sts remain.*
Round 98: *P1, k1 tbl, k2, k1 tbl, p1, k1 tbl; rep from * to end.

Move to step 3.

3 CAST OFF AND FINISHING
Cast off all sts loosely. Weave in all ends but do not trim.

Block cowl to measurements, following the instructions on pages 17–18.

Once dry, trim the remaining ends.

TECHNIQUE
CATCHING FLOATS

The secret to even stranded colourwork is in the floats. Floats are the strands of yarn that run along the back of your work – the yarn not in use is carried like this, until you need it again.

If the floats are too tight[1], the fabric becomes puckered, and if the floats are too loose[2], they may snag when you are wearing the item, and that will pull your stitches out of shape. When the floats are just right[3], they sit flat against the rear of the work, and the front of the knitted fabric is smooth.

When you are knitting a stranded motif where each colour is worked for a few stitches before switching, then the yarn not in use can simply be stranded along the rear and left to float. However, some patterns require the yarn to be carried for more than a few stitches, and the question then becomes, how many stitches should I work before catching in my float on the wrong side? This is a matter of functionality, as well as a matter of personal taste.

On the subject of functionality, a mitten for a small child (with small fingers), would be a situation where I would catch in the floats regularly. This avoids having strands of yarn that could snag in those small fingers. But on a cushion cover, where the wrong side won't be regularly touched, I would leave much longer floats of yarn, as that keeps the fabric more even.

As a rule of thumb (and you may feel differently!), I carry 4ply woolly yarns very happily behind 8 or 9 stitches without catching the float, in a situation where the rear of the work won't be exposed. Where the wrong side will be in use, such as on Janette Budge's Variance Hat, I would catch in the yarn not in use for stretches of 6 or 7 stitches or longer. In general, the stickier the yarn, the longer I will carry it (since it will felt into the rear of the fabric and therefore not catch anyway). And the thinner the yarn, the more stitches I will strand without catching. This is simply due to the size of the stitches – thicker yarn means larger stitches and therefore longer floats.

The longer your float, the harder it is to maintain a nice, even tension across the fabric. It can be helpful to catch in your yarn behind a stitch to break up a long float, and this can be repeated for extra-long stretches of stitches in one colour.

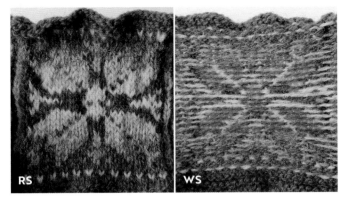

1 Floats are too tight.

2 Floats are too loose.

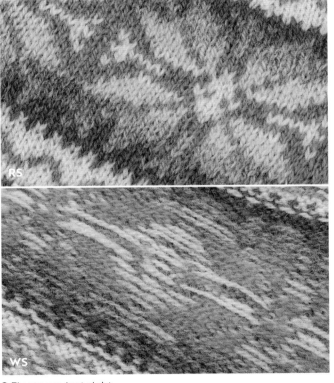

3 Floats are just right.

May

VARIANCE HAT – SHOWING TWO REPEATS OF CHART C

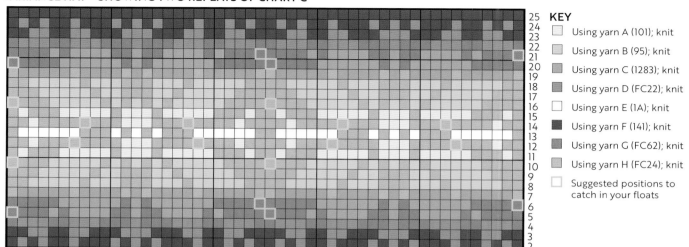

KEY

☐	Using yarn A (101); knit
☐	Using yarn B (95); knit
☐	Using yarn C (1283); knit
☐	Using yarn D (FC22); knit
☐	Using yarn E (1A); knit
☐	Using yarn F (141); knit
☐	Using yarn G (FC62); knit
☐	Using yarn H (FC24); knit
☐	Suggested positions to catch in your floats

In Janette's lovely Variance Hat, on row 5 of chart C the background yarn is worked for a stretch of 8 stitches (4 stitches at the start of the chart and another 4 at the end), so I would suggest catching it in on the 4th stitch of each stretch (which will be the last stitch of the chart).

Try to avoid catching in your yarn behind your work on the same stitch as you did on the row below as it will increase the chance that the wrong colour peeps through[4]. On row 6 of chart C there is a stretch of 10 stitches in yarn F (5 at each end of the chart), and you should catch in the yarn on the 6th stitch of each stretch, which will be the first stitch of the chart. That ensures that you don't catch the yarn on the same stitch column as the row below.

This version of chart C (above) shows two repeats of the motif, so that you can see the longer stretches of each colour more easily. I have marked up suggested positions for catching in your yarns that will avoid catching them on consecutive rounds in the same column.

Once you are in the flow of stranded colourwork, you will find a rhythm to catching the floats (or not!) that works best for you. The following tutorials will show you how to catch your floats behind the working yarn, without disrupting the flow of your knitting.

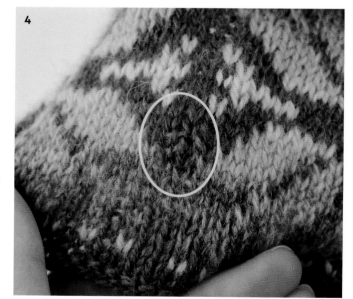

4

HOLDING YARNS FOR STRANDED COLOURWORK

It is a good idea to be consistent in how you hold your yarns when working stranded designs. It can help to maintain even tension, and you will find a full video tutorial on this subject over on our website (**www.acknitwear.co.uk/ confident-knitting**).

The tutorials below demonstrate catching floats with both yarns in your right hand as well as with one yarn in each hand.

Both of these options keep the yarns consistent and prevents them from tangling.

In all of the following tutorials, the green yarn is the background colour and the pink is the pattern colour.

WITH BOTH YARNS HELD IN THE RIGHT HAND: TO CATCH IN THE PATTERN COLOUR BEHIND THE BACKGROUND COLOUR
The background colour is over my index finger and the pattern colour is over my middle finger.

1 Work roughly half of the stitches in the background colour, using your index finger. Insert your right needle tip into the next stitch.

2 Bring the yarn not in use (the pattern colour) over the top of the right needle tip, and underneath.

3 Wrap the background colour around the right needle tip as if to knit as normal.

4 Bring the pattern colour back over the right needle tip, unwrapping it. You will see it is now caught behind the background colour.

5 Complete the stitch in the background colour. You will see that the pattern colour is caught between the fourth and fifth stitches.

6 Continue to work in pattern. Your pattern colour float has been caught at the rear of the work, and it has not tangled the yarns in any way.

May

WITH BOTH YARNS HELD IN THE RIGHT HAND: TO CATCH IN THE **BACKGROUND** COLOUR BEHIND THE **PATTERN** COLOUR

1 Work roughly half of the stitches in the pattern colour, using your middle finger. Insert the needle tip into the next stitch.

2 Wrap the background colour yarn around the needle tip as if to knit.

3 Then wrap the pattern colour yarn around the needle tip as normal.

4 Unwrap the background colour yarn and it will be caught in behind the pattern colour stitch.

5 Pull through the loop of pattern colour yarn to complete the stitch.

6 Continue to work in pattern. Your background colour float has been caught in at the rear without tangling.

HOLDING ONE YARN IN EACH HAND: TO CATCH THE **PATTERN** COLOUR BEHIND THE **BACKGROUND** COLOUR
The pattern colour is over my left index finger and the background colour is over my right index finger.

1 Work roughly half of the stitches in the background colour, using your right index finger. Insert the right needle tip into the next stitch.

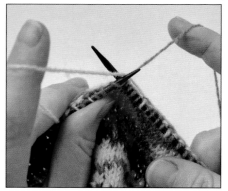

2 Swing your left index finger towards you, so that the pattern colour yarn is at the front of the work.

3 Knit the stitch using the background colour, with the pattern colour still towards you.

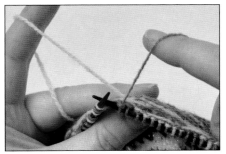

4 Once the stitch is complete, bring your left index finger back to its original position.

5 Complete the remaining background colour stitches. The pattern colour has been caught in.

HOLDING ONE YARN IN EACH HAND: TO CATCH THE **BACKGROUND** COLOUR BEHIND THE **PATTERN** COLOUR

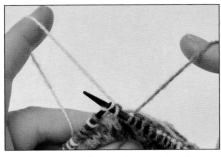

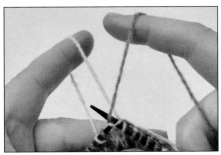

1 Work roughly half the stitches in the pattern colour, using your left index finger.

2 Insert your right needle tip into the next stitch as normal.

3 Use your right index finger to wrap the background colour around the tip as if to knit.

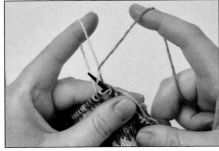

4 Use your left index finger to wrap the pattern colour around the tip as if to knit.

5 Use your right index finger to unwrap the background colour from the needle tip (it should now be caught at the base of the stitch you are working).

6 Pull the pattern colour yarn through the stitch to complete it as normal.

7 LEFT: Your background colour has now been caught behind the pattern colour.

I hope that these tutorials will allow you to catch your yarns in a smoother way, without interrupting the flow of your knitting. Janette's Variance Hat will give you the opportunity to practise catching your floats, and grow your confidence in stranded colourwork.

PROJECT
VARIANCE HAT

by Janette Budge

*The bold, traditional Shetland star motifs
of this glowing hat provide an opportunity
to practise catching your floats.*

SIZES

Small (Medium, Large, XL)
To fit head circumference: 45 (51, 57, 65) cm [17¾ (20, 22½, 25½) in]
Hat circumference at brim: 41.5 (50, 54, 62.5) cm [16½ (19¾, 21¼, 24½) in]
Length from brim to crown: 22.5 (22.5, 24.5, 24.5) cm [9 (9, 9½, 9½) in]
Circumference at widest point: 46.5 (55.5, 65, 74) cm [18¼ (21¾, 25½, 29¼) in]
Shown in size Medium on head circumference 55cm [21½in].

YARN

Jamieson & Smith 2ply Jumper Weight (4ply weight/fingering; 100% Shetland wool; 115m per 25g ball)
Yarn A: Shade 101; 1 x 25g ball in all sizes
Yarn B: Shade 95; 1 x 25g ball in all sizes
Yarn C: Shade 1283; 1 x 25g ball in all sizes
Yarn D: Shade FC22; 1 x 25g ball in all sizes
Yarn E: Shade 1A; 1 x 25g ball in all sizes
Yarn F: Shade 141; 1 x 25g ball in all sizes
Yarn G: Shade FC62; 1 x 25g ball in all sizes
Yarn H: Shade FC24; 1 x 25g ball in all sizes

Approximate yardages
Yarn A: 55 (65, 85, 95) m [60 (75, 90, 105) yds]
Yarn B: 20 (20, 25, 30) m [20 (20, 25, 30) yds]
Yarn C: 20 (20, 25, 30) m [20 (20, 25, 30) yds]
Yarn D: 15 (20, 25, 25) m [20 (20, 25, 30) yds]
Yarn E: 10 (10, 15, 15) m [10 (15, 15, 20) yds]
Yarn F: 35 (40, 50, 55) m [35 (45, 55, 60) yds]
Yarn G: 30 (35, 45, 50) m [35 (40, 50, 55) yds]
Yarn H: 35 (40, 50, 60) m [40 (45, 55, 65) yds]

NEEDLES AND NOTIONS

1 set 2.5mm [US 1.5] circular needles, 40cm [16in] long (for brim), or your preferred needles for working small circumferences in the round, or size needed to match corrugated rib tension
1 set 3mm [US 2] circular needles, 40cm [16in] long (for body of hat), or your preferred needles for working small circumferences in the round, or size needed to match stranded colourwork pattern tension
1 set 3mm [US 2] double-pointed needles (for crown shaping), or your preferred needles for working small circumferences in the round, or size needed to match stranded colourwork pattern tension
Stitch marker; Tapestry needle
Pompom maker or card for making a pompom (optional)

TENSION

27 sts and 31 rounds to 10cm [4in] over stranded colourwork pattern on larger needles, after washing and blocking
24 sts and 35 rounds to 10cm [4in] over corrugated rib pattern on smaller needles, after washing and blocking

ABBREVIATIONS

A full list of abbreviations can be found on page 112.

SPECIAL TECHNIQUES

Catching floats (pages 27–29)

The following video tutorials can be found on our website at
www.acknitwear.co.uk/confident-knitting
Catching floats with both yarns held in the right hand
Catching floats holding one yarn in each hand
Catching floats holding both yarns in the left hand
Colour dominance in Fair Isle
Splicing yarns together
Knitting in ends

PATTERN NOTES

This hat begins with a corrugated ribbed brim, followed by a classic stranded colourwork pattern, with peerie patterns before and after. The crown shaping echoes the main motif, with repeated decreases neatly forming a Shetland star.

The pattern is provided in four sizes, but if you wish to make further adjustments, here are some suggestions. To alter the depth, knit the ribbed brim to a different length. If you wish to alter the depth of the colourwork section, add to or remove the plain rounds between charts A, B and C. The easiest way to alter the circumference is to use a smaller or larger needle or a different weight of yarn, but you will need to work a swatch to be sure you are getting a fabric that you like, and then calculate what size of hat you will make using your new tension information.

HAT

1 CAST ON AND WORK BRIM

Using smaller needles and yarn A, cast on 100 (120, 130, 150) sts. Join to work in the round, being careful not to twist. Pm for start of round.

Round 1: Using yarn A, *k1, p1; rep from * to end.
Round 2: Work across 2 sts from row 1 of chart A for your size 50 (60, 65, 75) times.
Last round sets chart A pattern. Continue to work from chart A, changing yarns as indicated, until chart row 7 (7, 13, 13) is complete.

2 MAIN HAT BODY

Change to larger needles.
Round 1: Knit in yarn A.

Sizes Small, Medium and XL

Round 2 (inc): Using yarn A, k2 (2, –, 4), [kfb, k4 (3, –, 2)] 19 (29, –, 47) times, kfb, k2 (1, –, 4). *20 (30, –, 48) sts inc; 120 (150, –, 198) sts.*

Size Large

Round 2 (inc): Using yarn A, kfb, k1, [kfb, k2] 42 times, kfb, k1. *44 sts inc; 174 sts.*

All sizes

Round 3: Reading from right to left, work across 6 sts from row 1 of chart B 20 (25, 29, 33) times.
Last round sets chart B pattern. Continue to work from chart B, changing yarns as indicated, until chart row 4 is complete.

Sizes Small, Large and XL

Round 7 (inc): Using yarn A, [kfb, k23 (–, 173, 98)] 5 (–, 1, 2) times. *5 (–, 1, 2) sts inc; 125 (–, 175, 200) sts.*

Size Medium

Round 7: Using yarn A, knit.

All sizes

Round 8: *K1F, k1A; rep from * to last 1 (0, 1, 0) sts, k1 (0, 1, 0)F.
Round 9: Reading from right to left, work across 25 sts from row 1 of chart C 5 (6, 7, 8) times.
Last round sets chart C pattern. Continue to work from chart C, changing yarns as indicated, until chart row 25 is complete.
Round 34: *K1F, k1A; rep from * to last 1 (0, 1, 0) sts, k1 (0, 1, 0)F.
Round 35: Knit using yarn A.
Round 36 (dec): Using yarn A, [k2tog, k23 (23, 173, 98)] 5 (6, 1, 2) times. *5 (6, 1, 2) sts dec; 120 (144, 174, 198) sts remain.*
Round 37: Reading from right to left, work across 6 sts from row 1 of chart D 20 (24, 29, 33) times.
Last round sets chart D pattern. Continue to work from chart D, changing yarns as indicated, until chart row 4 is complete.

Size Small

Round 41: Using yarn A, knit.

Sizes Medium, Large and XL

Round 41 (dec): Using yarn A, k– (17, 8, 5), [k2tog, k– (34, 10, 9)] – (3, 13, 17) times, k2tog, k– (17, 8, 4). *– (4, 14, 18) sts dec; – (140, 160, 180) sts remain.*

All sizes

Move to step 3.

3 CROWN SHAPING

As crown gets smaller, switch to DPNs (or your preferred needles for working small circumferences in the round) when required, to work comfortably around hat.

Round 1: Reading from right to left, work across 20 sts from row 1 of chart E 6 (7, 8, 9) times.
Last round sets chart E pattern. Continue to work from chart E, changing yarns and decreasing as indicated until chart row 23 is complete. *108 (126, 144, 162) sts dec; 12 (14, 16, 18) sts remain.*
Break both yarns, leaving 10cm [4in] tails.

4 FINISHING

Thread the tails onto a tapestry needle and pass both tails together through the remaining stitches to secure. Push the needle through the centre of the crown and weave in the ends on the inside of the hat.
Weave in all remaining ends. Soak your hat in lukewarm water with wool wash for 20 minutes. Squeeze out the excess water. Lay flat to dry, taking care not to overstretch the ribbing, or dry over a hat form or balloon, or stuff with plastic bags. Leave to dry. If desired, make a pompom and attach firmly to the crown of the hat.

CHARTS

CHART E

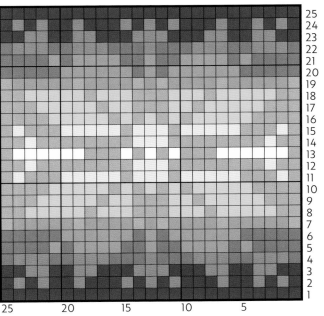

CHART NOTES
The hat is worked in the round, so all chart rows are read from right to left.

A monochrome chart with shade guide can be found on pages 34–35.

KEY

☐	Using yarn A (101); knit
☐	Using yarn B (95); knit
☐	Using yarn C (1283); knit
☐	Using yarn D (FC22); knit
☐	Using yarn E (1A); knit
■	Using yarn F (141); knit
☐	Using yarn G (FC62); knit
☐	Using yarn H (FC24); knit
•	Using shade indicated; purl
⋋	Using shade indicated; sl 1, k2tog, psso

CHART C

CHART D

CHART B

CHART A:
Large & XL

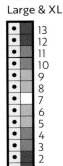

CHART A:
Small & Medium

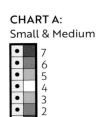

May

CHART A: SMALL AND MEDIUM

Chart Row	Background Colour	Pattern Colour
1	A	F
2	A	G
3	A	H
4	A	E
5	A	H
6	A	G
7	A	F

CHART A: LARGE AND XL

Chart Row	Background Colour	Pattern Colour
1 & 2	A	F
3 & 4	A	G
5 & 6	A	H
7	A	E
8 & 9	A	H
10 & 11	A	G
12 & 13	A	F

CHARTS B AND D

Chart Row	Background Colour	Pattern Colour
1	A	H
2	A	G
3	A	H
4	A	–

CHART C

Chart Row	Background Colour	Pattern Colour
1 & 25	F	–
2 & 24	F	D
3 & 23	F	D
4 & 22	G	D
5 & 21	G	C
6 & 20	G	C
7 & 19	H	C
8 & 18	H	B
9 & 17	H	B
10 & 16	H	B
11 & 15	H	A
12 & 14	H	A
13	H	E

CHART E

Chart Row	Background Colour	Pattern Colour
1	F	G
2–5	F	D
6	F	C
7–9	G	C
10	G	B
11–13	H	B
14	H	A
15–17	G	A
18	G	E
19–23	F	E

All yarns are Jamieson & Smith 2ply Jumper Weight

Original Colourway
Yarn A: Shade 101
Yarn B: Shade 95
Yarn C: Shade 1283
Yarn D: Shade FC22
Yarn E: Shade 1A
Yarn F: Shade 141
Yarn G: Shade FC62
Yarn H: Shade FC24

Alternative Colourway
Yarn A: Shade 203
Yarn B: Shade 27
Yarn C: Shade FC61
Yarn D: Shade 366
Yarn E: Shade 1A
Yarn F: Shade 36
Yarn G: Shade 21
Yarn H: Shade FC41

CHARTS

CHART NOTES
The hat is worked in the round, so all chart rows are read from right to left.

CHART E

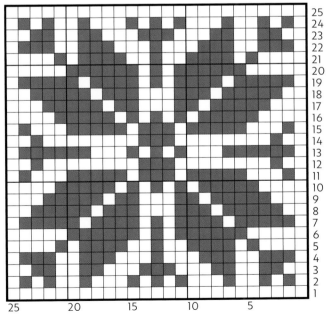

KEY

■ Using pattern colour; knit

□ Using background colour; knit

⊡ Using shade indicated; purl

⋏ Using shade indicated; sl 1, k2tog, psso

CHART C

CHART D

CHART B

CHART A:
Large & XL

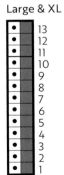

CHART A:
Small & Medium

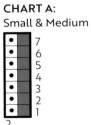

Summer

June

TECHNIQUE	**Embroidering Your Knitting**
PROJECT	**Patina Scarf**
DESIGNER	**Jeanette Sloan**

July

TECHNIQUE	**Vikkel Braids**
PROJECT	**Burnish Mittens**
DESIGNER	**Lily Kate France**

August

TECHNIQUE	**Reversible Cables**
PROJECT	**Lustrous Shawl**
DESIGNER	**Noma Ndlovu**

TECHNIQUE
EMBROIDERING YOUR KNITTING

I have to admit that embroidery is a technique that in the past, I have found a bit intimidating. I think it stems from the fact that you don't do the technique with knitting needles! If it feels outside of your comfort zone too, then don't worry – it turns out that you can embellish your knitting in spectacular ways with very little effort.

The turning point for me was seeing a few incredibly beautiful knitted projects that had been taken to a whole other level with embroidery. I knew I had to overcome my hesitancy and gain confidence with a sewing needle. Jeanette Sloan's Patina Scarf is the perfect example of a design that is breathtaking, and yet manageable if you take it step by step.

Set yourself up for success by putting aside a bit of time when you can experiment without interruptions. It is also a good idea to get comfortable with the idea that you might want to unpick your stitches a few times before you are happy with them. I'm not advocating a quest for perfection – the embroidery on this project benefits from some freestyling – rather I'm just acknowledging that you might try a couple of times before you master the tension and stitch size that looks best to you. Having the confidence to get it wrong and try again is all part of the journey.

ADDING GRID LINES

You can dive in with the embroidery straight away, but if you would like a bit of help to ensure that you keep the rough scale of the motifs on the Patina Scarf, you may find it helpful to add some grid lines in waste yarn. These will then relate to the grid lines on the embroidery chart found on page 45 of the pattern.

1 Thread a tapestry needle with waste yarn in a contrasting colour to your scarf. Follow a line of stitches halfway between your locking stitch markers, and sew a running stitch along this horizontal line.

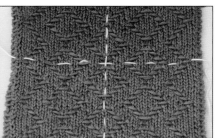

2 Repeat the process to mark a vertical line halfway across the scarf. This waste yarn cross will help to locate each embroidered motif. Once you have finished the embroidery, remove the waste yarn grid lines. You may need to carefully snip them out if the yarn has been pierced by any embroidered stitches.

DETACHED CHAIN STITCHES

Use yarn held doubled throughout. The detached chain stitch is also called lazy daisy stitch. This stitch is used for the central ring of the flower and each cluster of petals.

1 Weave in the end on the WS.

2 Make a small knot (on the WS).

3 Bring needle through fabric to RS at base of petal. Pull yarn gently until it is taut (but not so hard that you pull the knot through to the RS).

4 Thread your needle back into the fabric in same spot and back up, 1cm [⅜in] away (leave needle in fabric).

5 Wrap the yarn around the needle, so that the yarn runs parallel to the needle and only crosses behind the needle tip.

6 Pull the needle through – this makes a loop, and the yarn secures it at one end.

7 Take the needle back down through the fabric, just above the petal, in order to secure it.

8 Repeat steps 3–7 to complete the next petal. Continue to work stitches in the same way as required. This shows three detached chain stitches.

June

TWISTED CHAIN STITCH STEMS
Twisted chain stitch is used for the stems.

1 Secure yarn on WS as in steps 1 and 2 of the detached chain stitch tutorial.

2 Bring needle through fabric to RS at base of stem. Pull taut.

3 Go back into the fabric slightly to the right of where the yarn came through before, and come back up 1cm [⅜in] away (leave the needle in the fabric).

4 Wrap the yarn around the needle so that it crosses over the needle, before passing behind the needle tip.

5 Pull the needle through, thus creating a twisted loop that is secured to fabric. This creates a base stitch for your stem.

6 Take the needle back down through the fabric, just to the right outside edge of the top of the loop, and bring the needle back up through the fabric approximately 1cm [⅜in] away. Leave the needle in the fabric.

7 Wrap the yarn around the tip of the needle so that it crosses over the top of the needle and then passes behind the tip.

8 Repeat steps 5–7 as required to create your stem. Ensure that the yarn crosses the needle in the same direction each time so that your row of twisted stitches twists the same way. At the end of the stem, pass the needle to the WS of the fabric, just outside the final stitch.

9 Your completed stem will look like this.

FRENCH KNOTS

French knots are used for the centre of the main flower motif, as well as for the tips of petals on each stem, and the base of each separate set of three petals.

1 Secure the yarn on the WS of the fabric as in steps 1 and 2 of the detached chain stitch tutorial.

2 Bring the needle through the fabric to the RS where you want to place your French knot.

3 Wrap the yarn around the needle tip clockwise, three times – keeping the wraps snug. The secret to neat knots is keeping the yarn under a bit of tension.

4 Tip the end of the needle down so that it passes back through the fabric to the WS, just to the side of where it came through in step 2. Keep tension in the yarn.

5 Pull the needle all the way through the wraps to the WS of the fabric.

6 Secure the yarn on the WS with a small knot.

7 Repeat steps 2–6 as required.

Once you have completed the main embroidered section at the folded end of the scarf, you could also add a small motif to the other end. This flower is created with three detached chain stitches and a French knot. It has been carefully placed inside the knitted woven slip stitch diamond on the fabric.

I hope that embroidering Jeanette's Patina Scarf will leave you wanting to experiment with adding embroidery to many more knitted projects. It is much easier than it looks!

PROJECT
PATINA SCARF

by Jeanette Sloan

*Embroidered flowers pop against the gentle
ombré of this timeless, textured scarf.*

SIZE
One size only
Width: 18.5cm [7¼in]
Length: 161cm [63½in]

YARN
Schoppel Wolle Gradient (DK weight; 100% wool; 260m per 100g ball)
Yarn A: Tea Ceremony / Teezeremonie (2249); 2 x 100g balls
Schoppel Wolle Zauberball (4ply / fingering weight; 75% superwash wool, 25% biodegradable nylon; 420m per 100g ball)
Yarn B: Autumn Is Timeless / Herbstzeitlos (2335); 1 x 100g ball

Approximate yardages
Yarn A: 520m [570yds]
Yarn B: Approximately 5m [6yds] in each of three different shades

NEEDLES AND NOTIONS
One pair 4.5mm [US 7] knitting needles
4.5mm [US H/8] crochet hook for provisional cast on
A small quantity of smooth waste yarn of approximately DK weight
Locking stitch markers
Tapestry needle

TENSION
21.5 sts and 38 rows to 10cm [4in] measured over woven slip stitch pattern, after washing and blocking

ABBREVIATIONS
A full list of abbreviations can be found on page 112.

SPECIAL TECHNIQUES
Photo tutorials for the following techniques can be found within this book:
Crochet provisional cast-on method (page 9)
Detached chain stitch (page 39)
Twisted chain stitch (page 40)
French knots (page 41)

The following video tutorials can be found on our website at
www.acknitwear.co.uk/confident-knitting
Crochet provisional cast-on method
Detached chain stitch
Twisted chain stitch
French knots
Grafting

CHART NOTES
The scarf is worked back and forth in rows so all odd-numbered, RS chart rows are read from right to left and all even-numbered, WS chart rows are read from left to right.

PATTERN NOTES
This design begins with a crochet provisional cast on. The body of the scarf is worked in a slip stitch pattern, where the yarn is carried at the right side of the work. This creates a woven effect on the right side, which is mirrored by a raised textured pattern on the wrong side of the fabric. Slipping two stitches at the beginning of each row creates a rolled finish down each long edge of the scarf.

Although it may look difficult, the embroidery is a combination of 3 basic techniques: detached chain stitch, twisted chain stitch and French knots. If, at this point, you feel the French knots are beyond your abilities they can easily be replaced with beads instead. In order to avoid puckering the fabric of the scarf, we recommend that you lay the scarf on a flat surface when you are adding the embroidery. And because it can be difficult to keep the back of the embroidery as tidy as the front, the cast-on edge is folded upwards and grafted in place, creating a deep hem through which the other end of the scarf can be inserted when the scarf is being worn.

YARN NOTES
Before starting work, look closely at your two balls of Gradient, and check which colour is in the centre of each ball. Decide which ball to use first by choosing the one that has the centre colour closest to the outer colour on the other ball. This will ensure that when you change from one ball to the next, you get a smooth transition.

When you are nearly at the end of ball no. 1, alternate 2 rows in each colour until you have transitioned onto the second ball. The Zauberball is used as a simple way to get a few different coordinating shades of yarn to use for the embroidery. Alternatively you could use small quantities of leftovers from other projects.

June

SCARF

1 CAST ON AND SET UP

Read the Yarn Notes before starting work.
Make a slip knot in the waste yarn and place it on the crochet hook. Then using the crochet provisional cast-on method (see page 9), cast on 41 sts onto the knitting needle. Work a few extra chain loops before breaking off, then secure yarn to prevent it from unravelling.

Change to yarn A.
Set-up row 1 (RS): Knit to end.
Set-up row 2 (WS): Sl2 wyif, purl to end.

Move to step 2 for charted instructions or step 3 for written instructions.

2 MAIN SCARF BODY – CHARTED INSTRUCTIONS

Row 1 (RS): Reading from right to left, work across 41 sts from row 1 of chart A.
Row 2 (WS): Reading from left to right, work across 41 sts from row 2 of chart A.
Last 2 rows set chart A pattern. Continue to work from chart A until chart row 16 is complete for the 43rd time (688 pattern rows worked). Do not break off yarn.

Move to step 4.

3 MAIN SCARF BODY – WRITTEN INSTRUCTIONS

Row 1 (RS): Sl2 wyib, k5, sl2 wyif, k3, sl1 wyif, k3, sl2 wyif, k5, sl2 wyif, k3, sl1 wyif, k3, sl2 wyif, k7.
Row 2 and all following WS rows: Sl2 wyif, purl to end.
Row 3: Sl2 wyib, k4, sl2 wyif, k3, sl3 wyif, [k3, sl2 wyif] twice, k3, sl3 wyif, k3, sl2 wyif, k6.

KEY

☐ Knit on RS, purl on WS
☑ Sl1 wyib on RS, sl1 wyif on WS
☒ Sl1 wyif on RS, sl1 wyib on WS

Row 5: Sl2 wyib, k3, sl2 wyif, [k3, sl2 wyif, k1, sl2 wyif] 3 times, k3, sl2 wyif, k5.
Row 7: Sl2 wyib, k2, [sl2 wyif, k3] 3 times, sl3 wyif, [k3, sl2 wyif] 3 times, k4.
Row 9: Sl2 wyib, k1, sl2 wyif, k3, sl2 wyif, k5, sl2 wyif, k3, sl1 wyif, k3, sl2 wyif, k5, [sl2 wyif, k3] twice.
Row 11: As row 7.
Row 13: As row 5.
Row 15: As row 3.
Row 16 (WS): As row 2.
Last 16 rows set woven slip stitch pattern. Continue to work in pattern until row 16 is complete for the 43rd time (688 pattern rows worked). Do not break off yarn.

Move to step 4.

4 I-CORD CAST OFF

Using the cable cast-on method, cast on 3 sts to the left needle tip (these are the 3 i-cord sts). 44 *sts*.
Now work i-cord cast off as follows:
*Knit the next 2 sts, then k2tog tbl (this joins one i-cord st to one of the scarf sts, thus casting off 1 st). Slip these 3 sts back to the left needle. Rep from * pulling yarn firmly across the back of the work as you work the first stitch each time, until only 3 sts remain.
Cast off remaining 3 sts. Break yarn and fasten off.

5 FINISHING

Weave in all ends. Carefully block or gently steam the scarf to finished measurements. Allow to dry or cool thoroughly before unpinning.

6 EMBROIDERY

Measuring upwards from the provisional cast-on edge, place a locking stitch marker in each side at 18cm [7in] and 36cm [14¼in] (you'll be placing the embroidery between these two markers). Thread a tapestry needle with yarn B held double, and using the embroidery chart as a guide, place embroidery as shown, taking care not to pull too tightly on the stitches as this can pucker the fabric of the scarf. You will find photo tutorials on each of the three stitches used on pages 39–41.

7 GRAFT HEM

Returning to the provisional cast-on edge, carefully unzip the waste yarn and return the main yarn sts to a spare needle.
Pick up 41 sts along the U-shaped sts on the WS of the marked row at 36cm [14¼in]. Fold the scarf at the first set of markers (18cm [7in]) so the wrong sides are facing and the back of the embroidery is covered. Using your preferred method, graft the cast-on sts to the picked-up stitches to create an invisible join. Weave in any remaining ends.

CHART A: Woven slip stitch pattern

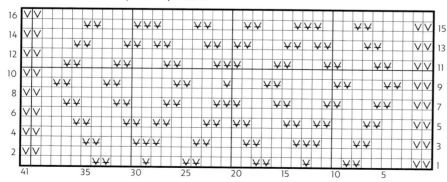

EMBROIDERY CHART

June

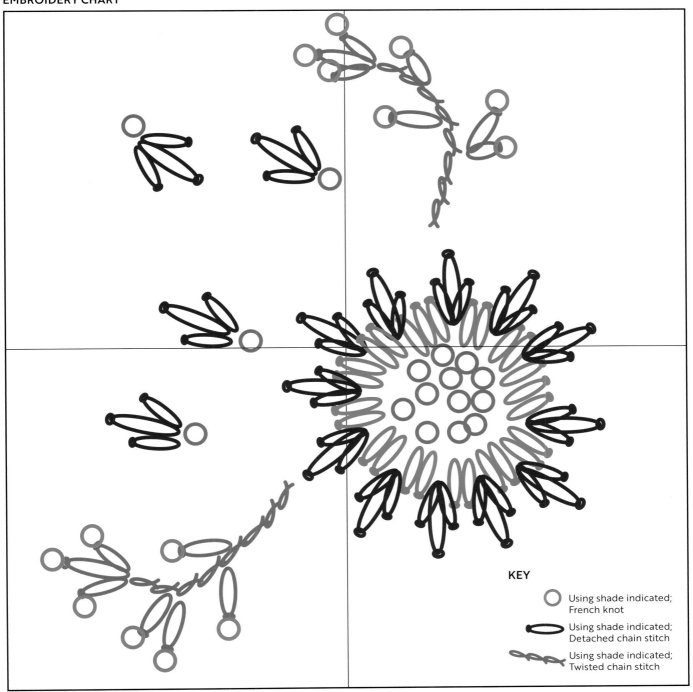

KEY

○ Using shade indicated;
French knot

⬮ Using shade indicated;
Detached chain stitch

⟳ Using shade indicated;
Twisted chain stitch

Embroidery chart is shown actual size - print at 100%.

TECHNIQUE
VIKKEL BRAIDS

Sometimes your knitted fabric needs an extra something to make a pattern pop, and a Vikkel braid is the perfect something! These braids create a round of horizontal stitches that add texture to your knitted fabric and can be used to great effect to frame other stitch patterns.

The basic braid manoeuvre is very similar to working a 1/1 LC cable – a 1 over 1 left cross cable, sometimes written as C2F. In essence, you just repeat the braid stitch over and over so that rather than creating a vertical cable, the braid travels horizontally around the cuff.

Do take care to ensure that your tension in the braid rounds matches the tension in the surrounding fabric. Some knitters may find it necessary to work their braids with a different size of needles to keep the fabric even.

The following tutorials include both one- and two-colour options, the latter allows you to work the horizontal braid in a different colour from the stitches for the following fabric. The tutorials below will take you through the process in detail.

SINGLE-COLOUR VIKKEL BRAID

1 Insert your right needle between the first two stitches on the left needle tip. Wrap your yarn around the right needle tip.

2 Pull the loop through.

3 Place the loop you pulled through on the left needle tip. You have cast on one stitch with the cable cast-on method.

4 Insert your right needle tip into the back of the second stitch on the left needle and wrap your yarn around the right needle tip.

5 Pull the loop through, but leave the original stitch on the left needle tip.

6 Knit the first stitch on the left needle as normal (into the front loop).

7 Slip both stitches off the left needle.

8 Slip the stitch just worked back to the left needle tip.

9 Repeating steps 4–8 will create the round of horizontal stitches that makes up the braid.

10 When the last stitch of the round is worked in step 4, complete steps 5–7. Break yarn and pull through the stitch just worked to fasten off.

11 Thread the tail onto a tapestry needle.

12 Pass the tapestry needle under both legs of the first horizontal braid stitch, under the left needle tip.

13 Pull the tail through so that the tension is similar to the adjacent stitches.

14 Insert the tapestry needle, from front to back, into the last horizontal braid stitch under the right needle tip.

15 Weave in the end on the wrong side. Once more fabric is knitted, the braid will sit neatly and horizontally around the cuff of the mitten.

July

TWO-COLOUR VIKKEL BRAID

In the following instructions, yarn B is the colour that you want to be visible in the horizontal braid, and yarn A is the colour that will be visible on the first round of stitches above the braid. To keep the braid neat, hold yarn A above yarn B.

1 Using yarn B, follow steps 1–3 from the single-colour braid tutorial to cable cast on one stitch to the left needle tip.

2 Insert your right needle tip into the back of the second stitch on the left needle and wrap yarn A around the right needle tip.

3 Pull the loop of yarn A through, but leave the original stitch on the left needle tip.

4 Knit the first stitch on the left needle as normal (into the front loop), using yarn B.

5 Slip both stitches off the left needle.

6 Slip the yarn B stitch just worked back to the left needle tip.

7 Repeating steps 2–6 will create the row of horizontal stitches that makes up the braid in yarn B, and the stitches on the needle will be in yarn A.

Follow steps 10–15 of the single-colour braid tutorial, breaking yarn B, in order to finish off the last stitch of your braid and thus create a seamless finish.

I hope that trying the Vikkel braids in Lily's Burnished Mittens will whet your appetite to explore the many other horizontal braids that you can create in knitting, such as the Latvian braid.

PROJECT
BURNISHED
MITTENS
by Lily Kate France

Tidy Vikkel braids and simple colourwork shine in these mittens, showing off the subtle shifts of hand-dyed yarn.

July

NEEDLES AND NOTIONS
1 set 2.5mm [US 1.5] needles of your preferred type for working small circumferences in the round, or size needed to match tension
Stitch markers
Small quantity of waste yarn
Tapestry needle

TENSION
40 sts and 44 rounds to 10cm [4in] over 3x1 rib pattern worked in the round, unstretched, after washing and blocking
40 sts and 44 rounds to 10cm [4in] over stranded colourwork pattern worked in the round, unstretched, after washing and blocking
You may need to use different needle sizes to get the same gauge in both stitch patterns. Please adjust accordingly, if required.

ABBREVIATIONS
A full list of abbreviations can be found on page 112.

SPECIAL TECHNIQUES
Photo tutorials for the following techniques can be found within this book:
Single-colour Vikkel braid (page 46)
Two-colour Vikkel braid (page 48)

The following video tutorials can be found on our website at
www.acknitwear.co.uk/confident-knitting
Vikkel braids
Grafting stitches or Three-needle cast-off method

PATTERN NOTES
The mittens start with a small rolled hem worked in stocking stitch, before the wrist is worked in rib. Two Vikkel braids are worked each side of a band of colourwork. The final Vikkel braid is worked as a two-colour braid in order to set up stitches in the main colour for the remainder of the mitten. The hand of the mitten is worked in 3x1 rib with a thumb gusset. The thumb stitches are left on hold while the remainder of the hand is completed. After shaping the top of the mitten the front and back stitches are joined by grafting or with a three-needle cast off. Finally, the thumb is completed in 3x1 rib with clean shaping at the top.

CHART NOTES
The mittens are worked in the round, so all chart rows are read from right to left.

SIZES
Small (Medium, Large, XL)
To fit hand circumference above thumb: 16 (18, 20, 22) cm [6¼ (7, 7¾, 8¾) in]
Actual hand circumference above thumb (unstretched): 12 (14, 16, 18) cm [4¾ (5½, 6¼, 7) in]
Length: 22 (27.5, 27.5, 32.5) cm [8½ (10¾, 10¾, 12¾) in]
Shown in size Large on hand circumference 20.5cm [8in].

YARN
Old Maiden Aunt Superwash Merino 4ply (4ply/fingering weight; 100% superwash merino wool; 365m per 100g skein and 73m per 20g skein)
Yarn A: Peachy Keen; 1 x 100g skein in all sizes
Yarn B: The White Hare; 1 x 20g skein in all sizes
Approximate yardages
Yarn A: 160 (235, 270, 355) m [175 (255, 295, 390) yds]
Yarn B: 60m [65yds] in all sizes

MITTENS
Make 2 alike.

1 CAST ON AND WORK CUFF
With yarn A, cast on 48 (56, 64, 72) sts. Join to work in the round, being careful not to twist. Pm for start of round.
Rounds 1–4: Knit.
Rounds 5–19: *K3, p1; rep from * to end.

2 COLOURWORK BAND AND BRAIDS
Work a single-colour Vikkel braid using yarn B (see page 46 for photo tutorial).
Work a single colour Vikkel braid using yarn A.
Round 1: Work across 4 sts from row 1 of chart A 12 (14, 16, 18) times.
Last round sets chart A pattern. Continue in chart A pattern, changing yarns as indicated, until chart row 1 has been worked for the 4th time (13 rounds of colourwork complete).
Work a single-colour Vikkel braid using yarn A.
Work a two-colour Vikkel braid using yarn B for the horizontal braid stitches and yarn A for the stitches that will be visible on your needles at the end of the braid (see page 48).
Next round: Using yarn A, *k3, p1; rep from * to end.
Repeat last round a further 4 times (5 rounds worked in 3x1 rib).
Move to step 3 for charted instructions and step 4 for written instructions.

3 THUMB GUSSET – CHARTED INSTRUCTIONS
Set-up round: Work 23 (27, 31, 35) sts in rib as set, pm, p1, pm, work remaining 24 (28, 32, 36) sts in rib as set.
Round 1 (inc): Work in rib to marker, slm, work across row 1 of chart B, slm, work in rib to end. *2 sts inc; 50 (58, 66, 74) sts.*
Last round sets chart B pattern. Continue in chart B pattern, increasing as indicated, until chart row 27 (33, 33, 39) is complete. *16 (20, 20, 24) sts inc; 66 (78, 86, 98) sts.*
Separate thumb as follows:
Next round: Work in rib to marker, remove marker, sl next 19 (23, 23, 27) sts to waste yarn, cast on 1 st using the backwards-loop method, remove marker, work in rib to end. *48 (56, 64, 72) sts.*
Move to step 5 for charted instructions or step 6 for written instructions.

4 THUMB GUSSET – WRITTEN INSTRUCTIONS
Set-up round: Work 23 (27, 31, 35) sts in rib as set, pm, p1, pm, work remaining 24 (28, 32, 36) sts in rib as set.
Round 1 (inc): Work in rib to marker, slm, M1R, p1, M1L, slm, work in rib to end. *2 sts inc; 50 (58, 66, 74) sts.*
Rounds 2–3: Work in rib to marker, slm, k1, p1, k1, slm, work in rib to end.
Round 4 (inc): Work in rib to marker, slm, M1R, k1, p1, k1, M1L, slm, work in rib to end. *2 sts inc; 52 (60, 68, 76) sts.*
Rounds 5–6: Work in rib to marker, slm, k2, p1, k2, slm, work in rib to end.

Round 7 (inc): Work in rib to marker, slm, M1R, k2, p1, k2, M1L, slm, work in rib to end. *2 sts inc; 54 (62, 70, 78) sts.*
Rounds 8–9: Work in rib to marker, slm, k3, p1, k3, slm, work in rib to end.
Round 10 (inc): Work in rib to marker, slm, M1R, k3, p1, k3, M1L, slm, work in rib to end. *2 sts inc; 56 (64, 72, 80) sts.*
Rounds 11–12: Work in rib to marker, slm, [p1, k3] twice, p1, slm, work in rib to end.
Round 13 (inc): Work in rib to marker, slm, M1R, [p1, k3] twice, p1, M1L, slm, work in rib to end. *2 sts inc; 58 (66, 74, 82) sts.*
Continue to work in pattern as set, increasing 1 stitch at each end of thumb gusset on every third round, until you have 19 (23, 23, 27) thumb sts between the markers. Take all increased stitches into 3x1 rib as set. Then work 2 more rounds without shaping. *8 (12, 12, 16) sts inc; 66 (78, 86, 98) sts.*
A total of 27 (33, 33, 39) thumb gusset rounds will have been worked.
Separate thumb as follows:
Next round: Work in rib to marker, remove marker, sl next 19 (23, 23, 27) sts to waste yarn, cast on 1 st using the backwards-loop method, remove marker, work in rib to end. *48 (56, 64, 72) sts.*
Move to step 5 for charted instructions or step 6 for written instructions.

5 HAND – CHARTED INSTRUCTIONS
Round 1: *K3, p1; rep from * to end.
Last round sets 3x1 rib. Continue to work in 3x1 rib with no further shaping until mitten measures 20 (25.5, 25.5, 30.5) cm [7¾ (10, 10, 12) in] from cast-on edge (no need to unroll the rolled edge when measuring).
Next round (dec): *Work across row 1 of chart C repeating the marked section 1 (2, 3, 4) times in total; rep from * once more. *4 sts dec; 44 (52, 60, 68) sts remain.*
Last round sets chart C pattern. Continue in chart C pattern, decreasing as indicated, until chart row 8 is complete. *28 sts dec; 16 (24, 32, 40) sts remain.*
Arrange the stitches so that the first 8 (12, 16, 20) sts of the round are on one needle, and the second set of 8 (12, 16, 20) sts are on a second needle. Hold the needles parallel with the tips pointing to the right, and the working yarn attached to the rear needle. Graft these sets of stitches together, or turn the mitten inside out and join them with a three-needle cast off. Move to step 7.

6 HAND – WRITTEN INSTRUCTIONS
Round 1: *K3, p1; rep from * to end.
Last round sets 3x1 rib. Continue to work in 3x1 rib with no further shaping until mitten measures 20 (25.5, 25.5, 30.5) cm [7¾ (10, 10, 12) in] from cast-on edge (no need to unroll the rolled edge when measuring).
Round 1 (dec): *Ssk, k1, p1, [k3, p1] 4 (5, 6, 7) times, k1, k2tog, p1, pm; rep from * once more. *4 sts dec; 44 (52, 60, 68) sts remain.*
Round 2 (dec): *Ssk, p1, [k3, p1] 4 (5, 6, 7) times, k2tog, p1, slm; rep from * once more. *4 sts dec; 40 (48, 56, 64) sts remain.*

Round 3: *Ssk, work in rib as set to 3 sts before marker, k2tog, p1; rep from * once more. *4 sts dec.*
Work last round a further 5 times. *24 sts dec; 16 (24, 32, 40) sts remain.*
Arrange the stitches so that the first 8 (12, 16, 20) sts of the round are on one needle, and the second set of 8 (12, 16, 20) sts are on a second needle. Hold the needles parallel with the tips pointing to the right, and the working yarn attached to the rear needle. Graft these sets of stitches together, or turn the mitten inside out and join them with a three-needle cast off.
Move to step 7.

7 THUMB
Return 19 (23, 23, 27) thumb sts to needles and rejoin yarn A.

Sizes Medium and Large only
Round 1: [K3, p1] 5 times, k3, pick up and knit 3 sts in gap at base of thumb. *26 sts.*
Pm and join to work in the round.
Round 2 (dec): [K3, p1] 6 times, p2tog. *1 st dec; 25 sts remain.*
Round 3 (dec): [K3, p1] 5 times, k3, p2tog. *1 st dec; 24 sts remain.*
Rounds 4–19: *K3, p1; rep from * to end.
Thumb should now measure 4.5cm [1¾in], i.e. 1cm [¼in] less less than desired thumb length. Work extra rounds of rib if a longer thumb is required.

Round 20 (dec): *Ssk, k1, p1, k3, p1, k1, k2tog, p1; rep from * once more. *4 sts dec; 20 sts remain.*
Round 21 (dec): *Ssk, p1, k3, p1, k2tog, p1; rep from * once more. *4 sts dec; 16 sts remain.*
Round 22 (dec): *Ssk, k3, k2tog, p1; rep from * once more. *4 sts dec; 12 sts remain.*
Round 23 (dec): *Ssk, k1, k2tog, p1; rep from * once more. *4 sts dec; 8 sts remain.*

Sizes Small and XL only
Round 1: K1, p1, [k3, p1] 4 (–, –, 6) times, k1, pick up and knit 3 sts in gap at base of thumb. *22 (–, –, 30) sts.*
Pm and join to work in the round.
Round 2 (dec): K1, p1, [k3, p1] 4 (–, –, 6) times, k1, k2tog, k1. *1 st dec; 21 (–, –, 29) sts remain.*
Round 3 (dec): K1, p1, [k3, p1] 4 (–, –, 6) times, k1, k2tog. *1 st dec; 20 (–, –, 28) sts remain.*
Rounds 4–19: K1, p1, *k3, p1; rep from * to last 2 sts, k2.
Thumb should now measure 4.5cm [1¾in], i.e. 0.5 (–, –, 1) cm [¼ (–, –, ½) in] less than desired thumb length. Work extra rounds of rib if a longer thumb is required.

Size Small only
Round 20 (dec): Ssk, k3, p1, k1, k2tog, p1, ssk, k1, p1, k3, k2tog, k1. *4 sts dec; 16 sts remain.*
Round 21 (dec): Ssk, k2, p1, k2tog, p1, ssk, p1, k2, k2tog, k1. *4 sts dec; 12 sts remain.*
Round 22 (dec): Ssk, k1, k2tog, p1, ssk, k1, k2tog, k1. *4 sts dec; 8 sts remain.*

Size XL only
Round 20 (dec): Ssk, [k3, p1] twice, k1, k2tog, p1, ssk, k1, [p1, k3] twice, k2tog, k1. *4 sts dec; 24 sts remain.*
Round 21 (dec): Ssk, k2, p1, k3, p1, k2tog, p1, ssk, p1, k3, p1, k2, k2tog, k1. *4 sts dec; 20 sts remain.*
Round 22 (dec): Ssk, k1, p1, k3, k2tog, p1, ssk, k3, p1, k1, k2tog, k1. *4 sts dec; 16 sts remain.*
Round 23 (dec): Ssk, p1, k2, k2tog, p1, ssk, k2, p1, k2tog, k1. *4 sts dec; 12 sts remain.*
Round 24 (dec): Ssk, k1, k2tog, p1, ssk, k1, k2tog, k1. *4 sts dec; 8 sts remain.*

All sizes
Break yarn, then using a tapestry needle thread yarn through remaining 8 sts and pull tight. Fasten off and weave in ends.

8 FINISHING
If you still need to finish off and weave in the end of the Vikkel braid, do so now.
Weave in all other ends but do not trim.
Soak your mittens in lukewarm water and wool wash for 20 minutes. Squeeze out excess water (but do not wring). Press between towels to dry further. Lay your mittens flat to dry, paying attention to fold them neatly along the thumb. When they are completely dry, trim any remaining ends.

CHARTS

CHART C: MITTEN TOP

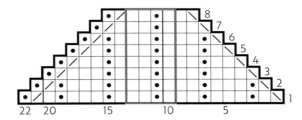

CHART B: THUMB GUSSET

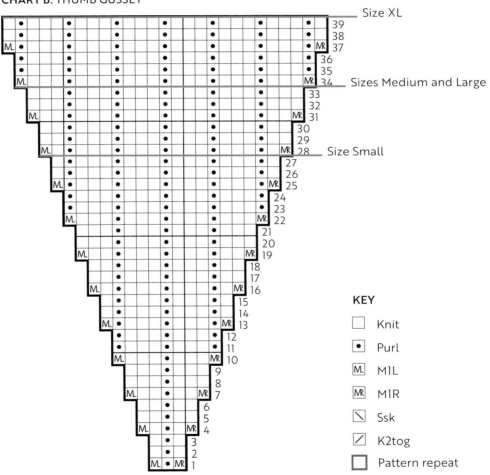

Size XL

Sizes Medium and Large

Size Small

KEY

☐	Knit
•	Purl
Ⓜ	M1L
Ⓜ	M1R
◲	Ssk
◳	K2tog
☐	Pattern repeat

KEY

■	Using yarn A (Peachy Keen); knit
■	Using yarn B (The White Hare); knit

CHART A: CUFF

TECHNIQUE
REVERSIBLE CABLES

Reversible cables are super cool! They combine the glorious texture of cables, with the versatility of a fabric that can be displayed with either side showing. This makes reversible cables perfect for scarves and shawls.

The basic premise of a cable is that, instead of working the stitches on your needles in the order in which they appear, you work the stitches out of order. The stitches are rearranged with the help of a cable needle, or by sliding them off the needle and rearranging when working without a cable needle. For wider cables though, it is generally a good idea to use a cable needle.

The simplest form of reversible cable is a "knit crossing purl" cable. When equal numbers of knit stitches cross over purl stitches, the RS of the cable looks the same as the WS. This can be used to manipulate a basic rib pattern very effectively. In the Lustrous Shawl by Noma Ndlovu, this principle is developed by crossing two sections of rib stitches over each other. By working k1, p2, k1 on each set of stitches that crosses, you create attractive columns of knit stitches moving on both sides of the fabric – these cables are abbreviated as 4/4 LRibC and 4/4 RRibC.

On the right side of the fabric, a k1, p2, k1 crosses over a second set of k1, p2, k1 stitches. The purl columns sink back into the fabric, leaving just the sinuous columns of knit stitches moving like twisted ropes.

On the wrong side of the fabric, the cable crosses appear as p1, k2, p1 crossing over each other. Again, the purl stitches sink back into the fabric (they are the knits on the other side of course), and the visible k2 columns twist round each other.

CONFIDENT KNITTING

WORKING A 4/4 LRIBC

1 Slip the next four stitches to a cable needle.

2 Hold the cable needle at the front of the work.

3 Bring the working yarn firmly across the back of the work and knit the first stitch on the left needle tip.

4 Purl the next two stitches from the left needle tip.

5 Knit the next stitch. You have now worked the four stitches that are crossing at the back of the work.

6 Knit the first stitch from the cable needle.

7 Purl the next two stitches from the cable needle.

8 Knit the last stitch from the cable needle. You have now completed the cable by working the four stitches that are crossing at the front of the work.

WORKING A 4/4 RRIBC

1 Slip next four stitches to a cable needle.

2 Hold the cable needle at the back of the work.

3 Bring the working yarn firmly across the work and knit the first stitch on the left needle tip.

August

4 Purl the next two stitches from the left needle tip.

5 Knit the next stitch. You have now worked the four stitches that are crossing at the front of the work.

6 Knit the first stitch from the cable needle.

7 Purl the next two stitches from the cable needle.

8 Knit the last stitch from the cable needle. You have now completed the cable by working the four stitches that are crossing at the back of the work.

The combination of garter stitch and reversible cables means that the finished Lustrous Shawl looks equally attractive on both sides.

PROJECT
LUSTROUS SHAWL

by Noma Ndlovu

Reversible cables and garter stitch create depth and drama in this statement shawl.

August

SIZE
One size only
Width at cast-on edge: 73.5cm [29in]
Length at unshaped row-end edge: 121.5cm [47¾in]

YARN
Fyberspates Vivacious DK (DK weight; 100% superwash merino; 230m per 115g skein)
Blueberry Imps (828); 3 x 115g skeins
Approximate yardage
685m [745yds]

NEEDLES AND NOTIONS
1 set 4.5mm [US 7] circular needles, 80cm [32in] long, or size to match tension (circular needles are recommended because of the number of stitches)
Stitch marker
Cable needle
Tapestry needle

TENSION
20 sts and 32 rows to 10cm [4in] over garter stitch, relaxed after washing and blocking
38 sts and 30 rows to 10cm [4in] over cable panel, relaxed after washing and blocking
It is vital to match the washed and firmly blocked tension here, or you may run short of yarn.

ABBREVIATIONS
4/4 LRibC Slip next 4 stitches to cable needle and hold at front, k1, p2, k1; then k1, p2, k1 from cable needle
4/4 RRibC Slip next 4 stitches to cable needle and hold at back, k1, p2, k1; then k1, p2, k1 from cable needle
A full list of abbreviations can be found on page 112.

SPECIAL TECHNIQUES
Photo tutorials for the following techniques can be found within this book:
Reversible cables (page 55)

The following video tutorials can be found on our website at
www.acknitwear.co.uk/confident-knitting
Reversible cables
Keeping track of cable rows

PATTERN NOTES
The Lustrous Shawl is cast on at the widest row. The shawl is worked in garter stitch and cables with regular decreases. This makes for a very enjoyable knitting experience as the project seems to speed up as you work!

You may find it helpful to place a locking stitch marker on the right side of the fabric after working a few rows, to help you to keep track of which is which. However, it is quite straightforward to work out, as the cable panel is at the start of right side rows, and at the end of wrong side rows.

As the recommended yarn is hand-dyed, we suggest transitioning from one skein to the next by working a section where you alternate skeins every two rows.

As the shawl is reversible, take care to weave in ends as invisibly as possible. Weaving in on the purl side of the cable ribs is a good option.

If you wish to make a larger shawl, simply cast on more stitches (in a multiple of 5) and work the extra stitches as part of the garter-stitch panel. Do ensure that you have enough yarn for this approach, as running out before you reach the end of the decreases would be frustrating!

It is also possible to adjust both the dimensions of the shawl by working at a different gauge, by changing your needle size or the weight of yarn chosen, but you will need to be sure that you are getting a fabric that you like and again, that you have sufficient yarn for this approach.

Instructions are provided in both written and charted forms.

SHAWL

1 CAST ON AND ESTABLISH PATTERN – CHARTED INSTRUCTIONS

For written instructions, move to step 2.

Using your favourite stretchy method (shown here with the long-tail cast on), cast on 185 sts.

Set-up row (WS): K105, pm, p1, *k2, p2; rep from * to last 3 sts, k2, p1.

Row 1 (RS, dec): [Reading from right to left, work across 16 sts from row 1 of chart] 5 times, slm, knit to last 4 sts, k2tog, k2. *1 st dec.*
Row 2 (WS): Knit to marker, slm, [reading from left to right, work across 16 sts from row 2 of chart] 5 times.
Last 2 rows set chart pattern with garter stitch and decreases on RS rows. Continue to work from chart as set until chart row 3 has been completed for the 21st time. *102 sts dec; 83 sts remain.*

Move to step 3.

CHART

KEY

□	Knit on RS, purl on WS
⊡	Purl on RS, knit on WS
⤬ (4/4 LRibC symbol)	4/4 LRibC; Slip next 4 stitches to cable needle and hold at front, k1, p2, k1; then k1, p2, k1 from cable needle.
⤬ (4/4 RRibC symbol)	4/4 RRibC; Slip next 4 stitches to cable needle and hold at back, k1, p2, k1; then k1, p2, k1 from cable needle.

CHART NOTES

The shawl is worked back and forth, so all RS, odd-numbered rows are read from right to left, and all WS, even-numbered rows are read from left to right.

2 CAST ON AND ESTABLISH PATTERN – WRITTEN INSTRUCTIONS

Using your favourite stretchy method (shown here with the long-tail cast on), cast on 185 sts.

Set-up row (WS): K105, pm, p1, *k2, p2; rep from * to last 3 sts, k2, p1.

Row 1 (RS, dec): K1, p2, *k2, p2; rep from * to 1 st before marker, k1, slm, knit to last 4 sts, k2tog, k2. *1 st dec.*
Row 2 (WS): Knit to marker, slm, p1, *k2, p2; rep from * to last 3 sts, k2, p1.
Rows 3–8: Work rows 1 and 2 a further 3 times. *3 sts dec.*
Row 9 (dec): [4/4 LRibC, 4/4 RRibC] 5 times, slm, knit to last 4 sts, k2tog, k2. *1 st dec.*
Row 10: As row 2.

Rows 1–10 set cable pattern with garter stitch and decreases on RS rows. Continue to work in pattern as set until row 3 has been completed for the 21st time. *102 sts dec; 83 sts remain.*

Move to step 3.

3 WORK DECREASES THROUGH THE CABLE PANEL
Next row (WS): K3, remove marker, p1, *k2, p2; rep from * to last 3 sts, k2, p1.

Throughout the following section keep the cable panel correct as set, working rib where there are insufficient stitches to work the final cable.

RS rows (dec): Work in established pattern to the last 4 sts, p2tog, k2. *1 st dec.*
WS rows: K2, work the remaining sts in established pattern. Repeat these 2 rows until 3 sts remain. *80 sts dec; 3 sts remain.*

Cast off loosely.

4 FINISHING
Weave in ends but do not trim. As the shawl is reversible, take care to weave in ends as invisibly as possible. Weaving in on the purl side of the cable ribs is a good option.

Soak your shawl in lukewarm water and wool wash for 20 minutes. Squeeze out excess water (but do not wring). Press between towels to dry further. Lay your shawl flat to dry, paying attention to keep all edges as straight as possible. When the shawl is completely dry, trim any remaining ends.

Autumn

September

TECHNIQUE	**Garter Stitch Short-Row Heel**
PROJECT	**Moorland Socks**
DESIGNER	**Jen Arnall-Culliford**

October

TECHNIQUE	**Mosaic Knitting**
PROJECT	**Terrain Mitts**
DESIGNER	**Marceline Smith**

November

TECHNIQUE	**Modular Knitting**
PROJECT	**Findhorn Wrap**
DESIGNER	**Emily K. Williams**

TECHNIQUE
GARTER STITCH SHORT-ROW HEEL

Knitting socks is endlessly satisfying to me. Turning a simple tube into a sock is a clever trick of engineering that's remarkably easy when you know how...

There are many options available to knitters for adding that bend in the tube that will accommodate your heel: in previous books we have covered the heel flap and turn, afterthought heel and toe-up gusset heel constructions.

This month we are exploring the garter stitch short-row heel. This is a particularly versatile heel construction as it is worked in exactly the same way whether you start your sock at the cuff or at the toe.

Short-row heels can of course be worked in stocking stitch, but I particularly like the extra stretchiness of this garter stitch version.

THE ANATOMY OF A SOCK
The stages of making a garter stitch short-row heeled sock are as follows:

CUFF
Stitches are cast on using a stretchy method. I generally use the long-tail cast on. The knitting is joined to work in the round, and the cuff is usually worked in a stretchy stitch pattern such as ribbing.

LEG
The leg is then worked in your choice of stitch pattern. We recommend a leg length of 16cm [6¼in] or shorter. Alternatively, if you want longer socks, you will need to cast on more stitches, then work some decreases down the leg to accommodate calf shaping.

HEEL
The heel is worked over approximately 55% of the total stitches. The heel is centred on the start of the round (so that the end you weave in at the cast-on edge will be at the back of the leg), so you work a partial round, leaving half of your desired heel stitches unworked. The heel is then worked back and forth across the old start of round.

A new length of yarn is joined in, so that the tails can be used to neaten the join later. The heel is then knitted back and forth over progressively shorter rows. A wrap and turn is used at the end of each row. The wraps are almost invisible amongst the loops of the garter stitch ridges, so there is no need to resolve them (or work them with the stitches when you come to knit back over them).

The shortest row that is worked determines the width of the back of the heel as well as the depth of the heel. Then in the second half of the heel, the rows get progressively longer until all heel stitches have been worked. The heel yarn is then broken off, leaving a tail to weave in later.

FOOT
Knitting in the round is begun again using the main yarn, and the foot is knitted until the desired foot length is achieved. The start of the round is placed at the side of the foot, to facilitate toe shaping. A stitch pattern may be used, but it is recommended that the sole stitches are kept in stocking stitch (or reverse stocking stitch) for comfort.

TOE
Decreases are worked to shape the toe before the stitches are grafted together to complete the sock.

GARTER STITCH SHORT-ROW HEEL

1 Work until you are at the start of the heel section. In the photo the top two needles hold the instep stitches, and the bottom two needles hold the heel stitches. The start of the round is at the join between the bottom two needles.

2 Using a new length of yarn, and leaving a tail to weave in later, knit across all but one of the heel stitches.

3 Bring yarn to front of work, between the needle tips.

4 Slip next stitch purlwise from left needle to right needle.

5 Return yarn to rear of work, between the needle tips.

6 Return the slipped stitch to the left needle without twisting it.

7 Turn, ready to work the next row, and take the yarn to the rear, between the needle tips. Steps 3–7 detail how to work the wrap and turn (w&t).

8 Knit to the first stitch of the heel.

9 Wrap this stitch, and turn (steps 3–7). You can see the wrap sitting at the base of the stitch.

September

10 Knit to the last unwrapped stitch.

11 Wrap this stitch, and turn (steps 3–7). It was the unwrapped stitch, and is now wrapped.

12 Continue to follow your pattern instructions until you have worked your shortest WS row.

13 On the next RS row, knit right up to the wrapped stitch.

14 Knit the wrapped stitch.

15 Bring yarn to front of work, between the needle tips.

16 Slip next stitch purlwise from left needle to right needle.

17 Return yarn to rear of work, between the needle tips.

18 Return the slipped stitch to the left needle without twisting it.

19 Turn, ready to work the next row, and take the yarn to the rear, between the needle tips.

Steps 15–19 show how to work a wrap and turn to create a double-wrapped stitch (the stitch being wrapped had already been wrapped in the first section of the heel).

CONFIDENT KNITTING

20 Knit to the first wrapped stitch.

21 Knit the wrapped stitch and then repeat steps 15–19 to double wrap the next stitch and turn.

22 Knit up to the double-wrapped stitch.

23 Knit the double-wrapped stitch.

24 Repeat steps 15–19 to double wrap the next stitch and turn.

25 Continue to work progressively longer rows, knitting the double-wrapped stitch, then creating the next double-wrapped stitch, until all heel stitches have been worked. On the final WS row, wrap the last stitch, but don't slip it back to the left needle.

26 Break the heel yarn, leaving a tail. Turn the work to the RS. Pick up the original yarn and knit across the heel stitches.

27 Continue to work the foot in the round. You can use the tails of the contrast yarn to neaten the corners of the heel if required.

The garter stitch short-row heel looks great paired with a contrasting coloured yarn, but can equally be worked in the same shade as the rest of the sock. However, it's advisable to use a separate length of yarn for working the heel, regardless of colour, in order to use the resulting tails to neaten the corners. I hope you will enjoy experimenting with colour combinations in my Moorland Socks pattern.

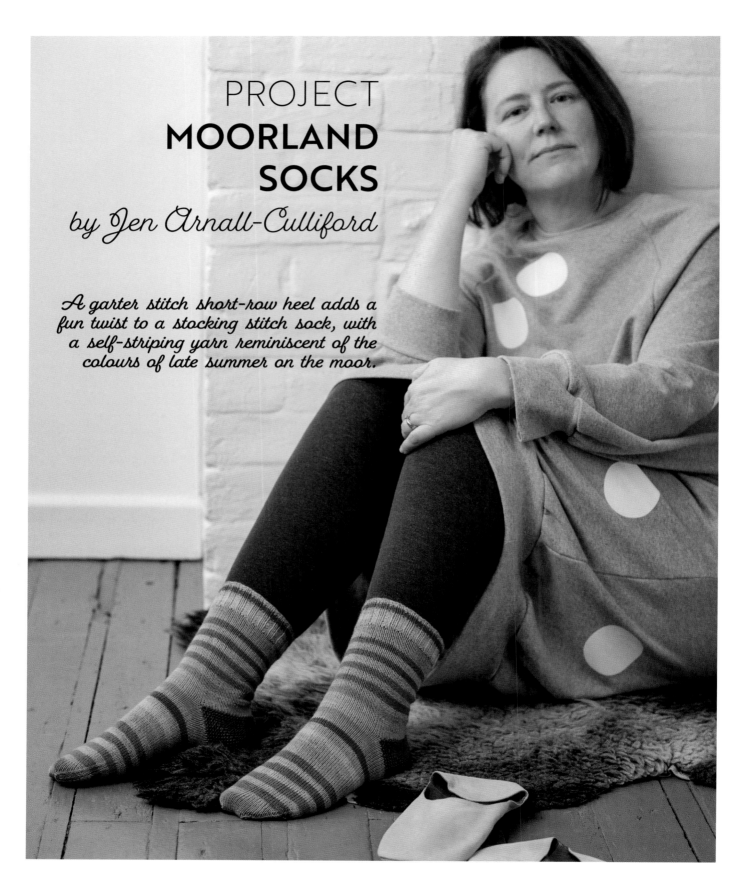

PROJECT
MOORLAND
SOCKS

by *Jen Arnall-Culliford*

A garter stitch short-row heel adds a fun twist to a stocking stitch sock, with a self-striping yarn reminiscent of the colours of late summer on the moor.

SIZES

Small (Medium, Large, XL, XXL)

To fit ankle and foot circumference: 19.5 (22, 24, 26, 28.5) cm [7¾ (8¾, 9½, 10¼, 11¼) in]

Actual ankle and foot circumferences of sock (unstretched): 15.5 (18, 20, 22, 24.5) cm [6 (7, 7¾, 8¾, 9½) in]

Length from cuff to top of heel: 16cm [6¼in]

Foot length and leg height are both fully adjustable within the pattern. Finished sock measures 0.5cm [¼in] less than actual foot length to ensure a good fit.

Show in size Large on ankle circumference 24cm [9½in] and foot circumference 22cm [8¾in].

YARN

Fab Funky Fibres Self-Striping Sock Yarn (4ply / fingering weight; 75% merino wool, 25% nylon; 2 x 40g plus 20g mini; 425m per 100g)

Yarn A: Feet Firmly on the Ground 2 x 40g self-striping skeins
Yarn B: Feet Firmly on the Ground 20g mini contrast shade

Approximate yardage

As the foot length is adjustable within the pattern, precise yardages are not possible. 400m [435yds] should be sufficient for all but the *very* longest XXL sizes.

NEEDLES AND NOTIONS

1 set 2.5mm [US 1.5] double-pointed needles or your preferred needles for working small circumferences in the round, or size to match tension
Stitch markers
Small quantity of waste yarn or stitch holder (optional)
Tapestry needle

TENSION

36 sts and 49 rounds to 10cm [4in] over stocking stitch in the round, after washing and blocking
36 sts and 70 rows to 10cm [4in] over garter stitch worked flat, after washing and blocking

ABBREVIATIONS

A full list of abbreviations can be found on page 112.

SPECIAL TECHNIQUES

Photo tutorials for the following techniques can be found within this book:
Garter stitch short-row heel (pages 63–65)

The following video tutorials can be found on our website at **www.acknitwear.co.uk/confident-knitting**
Long-tail cast on for DPNs
Garter stitch short-row heel
Grafting

PATTERN NOTES

These socks are worked from the cuff down. The cuff is worked in rib, followed by a stocking stitch leg. The contrast yarn is used to work a garter stich short-row heel, before the main yarn is used again to work the foot in stocking stitch. The sock is completed with a stocking stitch wedge toe and the stitches are grafted together for a seamless finish.

The short-row heel is worked over slightly more than half of the stitches, in order to give a good fit.

The pattern instructions include notes on using the stripes in the yarn to ensure that your socks match.

When choosing which size to make, measure both your ankle and foot circumferences. Ankle circumference is measured just above the ankle joint. Foot circumference should be measured around the arch of the foot. Select a To Fit size that matches the larger of these two measurements. You should then double check that the actual finished size of the sock will be slightly less than either your ankle or foot circumference. If you have a large difference between your ankle and foot circumferences, choose a size to fit the larger one, and then use smaller needles to adjust the tension and thus the size of the smaller area.

The foot length and leg height of your socks are easily adjusted within the pattern. If you require a smaller or larger circumference, you can cast on a different number of stitches (a multiple of 4). You will also need to adjust how many stitches are worked in the heel. See the garter stitch short-row heel tutorial for more information.

SOCKS
Make 2 alike.

1 CAST ON AND WORK CUFF
Using yarn A, cast on 56 (64, 72, 80, 88) sts. To ensure consistent stripes on both socks, start your cast on at a colour change in the yarn. You can then start your second sock at the same point. Join to work in the round, being careful not to twist. Pm for start of round.

Rib round: *K2, p2; rep from * to end.
Work rib round a further 20 times (21 rounds). Alternatively, work in rib until you have completed 5 stripes.

2 WORK LEG AND SHORT-ROW HEEL
Knit all rounds until your sock measures 16cm [6¼in] from cast-on edge. Make a note of which colour stripe you are on, and how many rounds have been worked in that shade. This will help you to match your second sock perfectly. Length can be adjusted here as desired, but be aware that longer socks would require some calf shaping.

Partial round: Using yarn A, k41 (46, 52, 57, 63).

You are now positioned at the start of the heel. The heel will be worked back and forth using yarn B (the contrast skein) only. Leave a tail of yarn B to weave in later. For more information on working the short-row heel, see tutorial on page 63.

Throughout the following section you will work progressively shorter rows, with stitches left unworked at each end.
Short row 1 (RS): Using yarn B, k29 (35, 39, 45, 49) removing start of round marker as you pass it, w&t. If desired, slip the remaining 26 (28, 32, 34, 38) instep sts, after the wrapped stitch, to a spare needle or waste yarn while the heel is worked.
Short row 2 (WS): K28 (34, 38, 44, 48), w&t.
Short row 3: K27 (33, 37, 43, 47), w&t.
Short row 4: K26 (32, 36, 42, 46), w&t.
Short row 5 (RS): Knit to last st before the wrapped st, w&t.
Short row 6 (WS): Knit to last st before the wrapped st, w&t.
Rep last 2 rows a further 8 (11, 13, 15, 17) times. Final WS row will be worked as k8 (8, 8, 10, 10), w&t.

Throughout the following section you will work progressively longer rows, with stitches left unworked at each end.
Short row 1 (RS): K8 (8, 8, 10, 10), knit the next stitch (this has been wrapped), w&t (you are adding a second wrap to a stitch that was previously wrapped).
Short row 2 (WS): K9 (9, 9, 11, 11), knit the wrapped stitch, w&t (adding a second wrap to a previously wrapped stitch).
Short row 3: K10 (10, 10, 12, 12), knit the double-wrapped stitch, w&t (this makes a double-wrapped stitch).
Short row 4: K11 (11, 11, 13, 13), knit the double-wrapped stitch, w&t (this makes a double-wrapped stitch).

Short row 5 (RS): Knit to the double-wrapped stitch, knit the double-wrapped stitch, w&t (this makes a double-wrapped stitch).
Short row 6 (WS): Knit to the double-wrapped stitch, knit the double-wrapped stitch, w&t (this makes a double-wrapped stitch).
Rep last 2 rows a further 7 (10, 12, 14, 16) times. Final WS row will be worked as k27 (33, 37, 43, 47), knit the double-wrapped stitch, then wrap the final stitch (which will be the first stitch of the heel) but don't return that stitch to the left needle. Turn work to RS. Break yarn B, leaving a tail to weave in later.

3 WORK FOOT AND TOE
If required, return the 26 (28, 32, 34, 38) instep sts to your needles.
Partial round: Using yarn A, k1 (2, 2, 3, 3).

Place new start of round marker. The start of the round is now at the side of the foot/toe. The remainder of the sock is worked in yarn A only.

Knit all rounds until your sock measures 3 (4, 4, 5, 5.5) cm [1 (1½, 1½, 2, 2) in] less than desired foot length, when measured from the base of the heel. Make a note of which colour stripe you are on, and how many rounds have been worked in that colour. This will help you to match your second sock.

Round 1 (dec): *K1, ssk, k22 (26, 30, 34, 38), k2tog, k1, pm; rep from * once more. 4 sts dec; 52 (60, 68, 76, 84) sts remain.
Round 2: Knit to end, slipping markers.
Round 3 (dec): *K1, ssk, knit to 3 sts before marker, k2tog, k1, slm; rep from * once more. 4 sts dec.
Repeat last 2 rounds a further 7 (9, 10, 12, 13) times. 32 (40, 44, 52, 56) sts dec; 20 (20, 24, 24, 28) sts remain.

Slip first 10 (10, 12, 12, 14) sts to one needle, and the remaining 10 (10, 12, 12, 14) sts to a second needle. Break yarn A, leaving a tail of 30cm [12in]. Hold both needles parallel with the tips pointing to the right, and graft the two sets of stitches together.

4 SECOND SOCK
Repeat steps 1–3 to make second sock, using your notes on which stripe you were on at each change in stitch pattern to ensure that your socks match neatly.

5 FINISHING
Weave in all ends but do not trim. Soak your socks in lukewarm water and wool wash for 20 minutes. Squeeze out excess water (but do not wring). Press between towels to dry further. Lay your socks flat to dry or stretch over sock blockers. When they are completely dry, trim any remaining ends.

TECHNIQUE
MOSAIC KNITTING

Mosaic knitting is one of the best knitting tricks you will come across. You create beautiful, complex-looking, colourwork fabrics, without ever using more than one colour at a time. It's no more difficult than stripes, and yet the stitch pattern possibilities are endless.

Mosaic patterns are created by working stripes, but instead of knitting (or purling) all stitches, some stitches are slipped. Rows or rounds with slipped-stitch patterning are worked in pairs, where the same stitches are slipped on the second row or round. This makes mosaic knitting very intuitive as you can work the second of each pair of rows or rounds without having to refer to the pattern instructions. Over the course of a pattern repeat, all columns of stitches will end up with the same number of stitches worked. For example, in Marceline Smith's beautiful Terrain Mitts, over the six-row pattern, each stitch is worked four times and slipped twice. When you slip stitches, the yarn is always held at the wrong side of the work (so the floats are kept on the wrong side). And that's really all there is to it! Mosaic knitting looks so much more complicated than it is.

MOSAIC KNITTING IN THE ROUND

1 Stitches are slipped purlwise with the yarn held at the back. If you are slipping more than one stitch, it may be easier to slip them together. Here, two stitches are being slipped together.

2 Knit the next stitch, ensuring that your stitches are spread out on the right needle, so that the float of yarn isn't too tight on the wrong side.

3 From time to time, take a look at your stitches just worked, and check that you are keeping an even tension – particularly behind the slipped stitches.

MOSAIC KNITTING WORKED BACK AND FORTH

1 On right side rows, slipped stitches are worked in the same way as when you were knitting in the round. The stitches are slipped purlwise with the yarn at the back.

2 Knit the next stitch, ensuring that your stitches are spread out on the right needle, so that the float of yarn isn't too tight on the wrong side.

3 On wrong side rows, the stitches are purled.

4 When slipping stitches, they are slipped purlwise, but this time the yarn is held at the front of the work, so that the floats remain on the wrong side.

5 When purling the next stitch, ensure that your stitches are spread out on the right needle, so that the float of yarn isn't too tight.

6 Here you can see that the purled stitches and the slipped stitches are spread out evenly and the float sits neatly at the wrong side.

CARRYING YARNS BETWEEN ROUNDS

As you would when working stripes, it is helpful to catch in yarns not in use at the start of the round. This helps to prevent long vertical floats forming at the rear of the work, and keeps tension more even. The following photo tutorial shows how to catch in one or two yarns not in use at the start of the round. If you are working a round using the same yarn as the previous round, there is no need to catch in the unused yarns in this way.

1 At the end of round 3 of the pattern used in the Terrain Mitts, yarn B has been used, and the next round will be worked with yarn C. Hold the old yarn (B) over the new yarn (C).

2 Then knit the first stitch of the new round with the new colour (here it is yarn C).

3 Later in the pattern when yarn A is introduced, you will hold both yarns not in use (yarns B and C) over the new yarn at the start of the round. This ensures that you aren't carrying the yarns too far vertically at the start of the round.

I hope you will have fun experimenting with mosaic knitting patterns in Marceline's pretty Terrain Mitts, and that you'll feel confident about trying mosaic stitch patterns in future projects. The Terrain Mitts use a pattern based on stocking stitch, but mosaic patterns also work brilliantly with garter stitch. There are so many possibilities!

PROJECT
TERRAIN MITTS

by Marceline Smith

Mosaic stitches and natural shades evoke shifting terrain for these striking fingerless mitts.

October

SIZES

Small (Medium, Large, XL)

To fit hand circumference above thumb: 15.5 (18.5, 21, 24) cm [6 (7¼, 8¼, 9½) in]

Actual hand circumference above thumb: 15 (18, 20.5, 23.5) cm [5¾ (7, 8¼, 9¼) in]

Length: 21.5 (22.5, 23.5, 24.5) cm [8½ (8¾, 9¼, 9¾) in]

Shown in size Medium on hand circumference 18cm [7in].

YARN

Jamieson & Smith Shetland Supreme Jumper Weight (4ply / fingering weight; 100% Shetland wool; 172m per 50g ball)

Yarn A: Shetland Black (2005); 1 x 50g ball
Yarn B: Shaela (2003); 1 x 50g ball
Yarn C: White (2001); 1 x 50g ball

Approximate yardages
Yarn A: 65 (80, 95, 115) m [70 (85, 105, 125) yds]
Yarn B: 75 (95, 115, 140) m [85 (105, 125, 150) yds]
Yarn C: 50 (60, 75, 90) m [55 (70, 85, 100) yds]

NEEDLES AND NOTIONS

1 set 2.5mm [US 1.5] circular needles, 80cm [32in] long for working magic loop, or your preferred needles for knitting in the round, or size needed to match 1x1 rib tension

1 set 3.25mm [US 3] circular needles, 80cm [32in] long for working magic loop, or your preferred needles for knitting in the round, or size needed to match mosaic pattern tension

Stitch marker

Tapestry needle

TENSION

26 sts and 40 rounds to 10cm [4in] over 1x1 rib in the round, using larger needles, after washing and blocking

27 sts and 57 rounds to 10cm [4in] over mosaic pattern in the round and worked flat, using larger needles, after washing and blocking

ABBREVIATIONS

A full list of abbreviations can be found on page 112.

SPECIAL TECHNIQUES

Photo tutorials for the following techniques can be found within this book:

Mosaic knitting (page 71)
Carrying yarns at the end of the round (page 72)

The following video tutorials can be found on our website at **www.acknitwear.co.uk/confident-knitting**
Mosaic knitting
Alternating cable cast on

PATTERN NOTES

These mitts are knitted from the bottom up with a ribbed cuff, thumb, and top edge. The main body of each mitt features a three-colour mosaic motif. The thumb opening is created by knitting the mosaic motif flat, and the ribbed thumb is made with stitches picked up from around the opening. The finished mitts include 0.5cm [¼in] of negative ease for all sizes.

The pattern is provided in four sizes, but if you wish to make further adjustments it will be straightforward to add or remove a multiple of four stitches to give a smaller or larger hand circumference. You can also very easily adjust the length by changing the number of repeats of the mosaic pattern both before and after the thumb opening. Any changes will of course affect the yarn requirements.

In a mosaic project using two or more colours, it is best to continuously carry the strands up the side or inside of the work. Whether the pattern is knitted flat or in the round, the technique recommended for managing yarns in this project is to hold the old yarn over the new yarn. This means that each time a new colour is to be used for the first time, the strand(s) of the previous colour(s) should be crossed over the top of the new colour, at the back of the work, then the new colour is used to continue in pattern. When three colours are in play, it is helpful to cross both colours that are not in use over the new colour so that the correct strand is always close at hand to be used. If you are using the same colour for a second row or round, you do not need to cross the strands a second time.

MITTS
Make 2 alike.

1 CAST ON AND WORK RIBBED CUFF
With smaller needles and yarn A, use the alternating cable cast on or your preferred method and cast on 32 (40, 48, 56) sts. Join to work in the round, being careful not to twist. Pm for start of round.

Rounds 1–3: *K1, p1; rep from * to end.

Break off yarn A. Change to larger needles and yarn B.
Rounds 4–20: *K1, p1; rep from * to end.

Round 21 (inc): *K3 (4, 5, 6), kfb; rep from * to end. *8 sts inc; 40 (48, 56, 64) sts.*
Do not break yarn B.

Move to step 2 for charted instructions or step 3 for written instructions.

2 WORK MOSAIC PATTERN – CHARTED INSTRUCTIONS
Round 1: Reading from right to left, work across 4 sts from row 1 of chart A 10 (12, 14, 16) times in total.
Last round sets chart A pattern. Continue to work from chart A, changing shades as indicated, until chart row 6 is complete for the 8th (8th, 9th, 9th) time (48 (48, 54, 54) rounds worked in mosaic pattern).

Move to step 4.

KEY
■ Using yarn A (Shetland Black 2005); knit

▨ Using yarn B (Shaela 2003); knit

☐ Using yarn C (White 2001); knit

Ⅴ Sl1 pwise wyib

KEY
■ Using yarn A (Shetland Black 2005); knit on RS, purl on WS

▨ Using yarn B (Shaela 2003); knit on RS, purl on WS

☐ Using yarn C (White 2001); knit on RS, purl on WS

Ⅴ Sl1 pwise wyib on RS, sl1 pwise wyif on WS

CHART A: working in the round

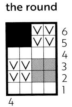

CHART B: working flat, Row 1 is WS

3 WORK MOSAIC PATTERN – WRITTEN INSTRUCTIONS
Round 1: Using yarn C, knit.
Rounds 2–3: Using yarn B, *k2, sl2 pwise wyib; rep from * to end.
Round 4: Using yarn C, knit.
Rounds 5–6: Using yarn A, *sl2 pwise wyib, k2; rep from * to end.
Last 6 rounds set mosaic pattern in the round. Continue to work in pattern until round 6 is complete for the 8th (8th, 9th, 9th) time (48 (48, 54, 54) rounds worked in mosaic pattern).

Move to step 5.

4 WORK THUMB OPENING – CHARTED INSTRUCTIONS
In the following section you will switch to working the mosaic pattern back and forth (flat). This creates the thumb opening. Remove the start of round marker, and turn, ready to work a WS row.
Row 1 (WS): Reading from left to right, work across 4 sts from row 1 of chart B 10 (12, 14, 16) times in total.
Row 2 (RS): Reading from right to left, work across 4 sts from row 2 of chart B 10 (12, 14, 16) times in total.
Last 2 rows set chart B pattern. Continue to work from chart B until row 4 is complete for the 3rd (4th, 4th, 5th) time (16 (22, 22, 28) rows of mosaic pattern worked flat). If row tension is correct, the opening should now measure 3 (4, 4, 5) cm [1 (1½, 1½, 2) in]. The thumb circumference will be double this, so adjust how many rows you work if desired.

Move to step 6.

5 WORK THUMB OPENING – WRITTEN INSTRUCTIONS
In the following section you will switch to working the mosaic pattern back and forth (flat). This creates the thumb opening. Remove the start of round marker, and turn, ready to work a WS row.
Row 1 (WS): Using yarn C, purl.
Row 2 (RS): Using yarn B, *k2, sl2 pwise wyib; rep from * to end.
Row 3: Using yarn B, *sl2 pwise wyif, p2; rep from * to end.
Row 4: Using yarn C, knit.
Row 5: Using yarn A, *p2, sl2 pwise wyif; rep from * to end.
Row 6: Using yarn A, *sl2 pwise wyib, k2; rep from * to end.
Last 6 rows set mosaic pattern worked flat. Continue to work mosaic pattern flat until row 4 is complete for the 3rd (4th, 4th, 5th) time (16 (22, 22, 28) rows of mosaic pattern worked flat). If row tension is correct, the opening should now measure 3 (4, 4, 5) cm [1 (1½, 1½, 2) in]. The thumb circumference will be double this, so adjust how many rows you work if desired.

Move to step 6.

6 WORK UPPER HAND

With RS facing you, resume working in the round. Pm for start of round.

Using yarn A, and beginning with round 5, work a further 15 rounds in mosaic pattern worked in the round, thus ending with round 1 of pattern.

Break off yarns A and C.
Rounds 1–7: Using yarn B, *k1, p1; rep from * to end.

Break off yarn B. Change to smaller needles and yarn A.
Rounds 8–10: *K1, p1; rep from * to end.
Cast off all sts loosely.

7 WORK THUMB

Using yarn B, smaller needles and with RS facing, begin at the bottom of the thumb opening and pick up and knit 8 (10, 10, 13) sts to top of thumb opening, then pick up and knit another 8 (10, 10, 13) sts down the other side to the bottom. *16 (20, 20, 26) sts.*
Join to work in the round. Pm for start of round.
Round 1: Knit all sts through the back loop.
Rounds 2–10: *K1, p1; rep from * to end.
Rounds 11–13: Using yarn A, *k1, p1; rep from * to end.
Cast off all sts loosely.

8 FINISHING

Weave in ends. Soak your mitts in lukewarm water with wool wash for 20 minutes. Squeeze out excess water. Lay flat to measurements, and allow to dry.

TECHNIQUE
MODULAR
KNITTING

A modular fabric is one consisting of multiple small geometric shapes. These shapes can be sewn or crocheted together, or as in Emily K. Williams's striking Findhorn Wrap they can be knitted on to each other. The fabrics created with modular knitting allow lots of scope to play with colour. The weaving style and palette of the artist Anni Albers were the inspiration behind the Findhorn Wrap, and you could easily experiment with different colour combinations.

Emily has chosen a twofold joining strategy for the Findhorn Wrap. The wrap is formed from four strips of knitting, with each strip consisting of 36 blocks. The blocks are joined to each other simply by changing colour and continuing to work on the live stitches. The strips are then joined using a versatile method where yarn overs are created on the edge of the fabric, and they are then picked up and knitted when the next strip is worked. This creates a decorative eyelet detail along the joined edges.

With yarn overs at the edge of a motif, you can easily join in many different shapes. The following photo tutorials will show you how to work a yarn over at the start of a row, before both knit and purl stitches. The next section will show how the yarn overs are picked up and knitted to join adjacent strips. And finally, we are including a tutorial on working the Russian join. As there are so many colour changes in this wrap, and the yarn isn't suitable for splicing, the Russian join is an excellent method for making near-invisible colour changes.

WORKING A YARN OVER AT THE START OF A ROW, BEFORE A KNIT STITCH

1 Hold the working yarn over the right needle tip, bringing the yarn from in front of the needle, over the top of the needle and to the rear of the work.

2 Insert the right needle into the first stich on the left needle. Here we are working a k2tog, so the right needle goes into the first two stitches on the left needle. You can see that the yarn is creating a yarn over before the next stitch is worked.

3 Wrap the yarn around the right needle tip and continue to work the stitch as normal.

WORKING A YARN OVER AT THE START OF A ROW, BEFORE A PURL STITCH

4 You can see that there is a yarn over on the right needle before the k2tog stitch (which was the first stitch of this row).

5 Working a yarn over at the start of the row creates a looped edge.

1 Hold the working yarn over the right needle tip, bringing the yarn from in front of the needle, over the top of the needle and to the rear of the work.

2 Continue to bring the yarn around the needle, passing between the needle tips, so that it wraps all the way around the right needle, and is now in position to purl.

3 Insert the right needle into the first stitch on the left needle. Here we are working a p2tog, so the right needle goes into the first two stitches on the left needle. You can see that the yarn is creating a yarn over before the next stitch is worked. The yarn is wrapped around the needle to work the stitch.

4 You can see that there is a yarn over on the right needle before the p2tog stitch (which was the first stitch of this row).

PICKING UP AND KNITTING A YARN OVER FROM THE BORDER ROW

At the start of strips 2, 3 and 4 in the Findhorn Wrap, you will pick up and knit a yarn over from the final row of the border. The following tutorial will show you how this is done.

1 Insert the left needle tip into the yarn over adjacent to the left needle tip (this yo was created on the last row of the border, and is already joined to the previous strip). Insert the needle from front to back, so that the right leg of the stitch is at the front of the needle.

2 Insert your right needle knitwise into the picked-up yarn over and pull through a loop of your new yarn, thus knitting the picked-up stitch.

3 Continue to work in pattern according to the instructions.

PICKING UP AND KNITTING A YARN OVER FROM THE ADJACENT STRIP

1 Insert your left needle tip, from front to back, into the adjacent yarn over from the previous strip. The yarn over sits on the needle with the right leg of the stitch at the front of the needle.

2 Insert your right needle into the picked-up stitch knitwise and wrap the yarn around to knit it as normal.

RUSSIAN JOIN

To achieve a clean colour change, the Russian join is a handy technique to use when your yarn isn't suitable for splicing (splicing only works on yarns that will felt). Work to the last six stitches, and then cut the yarn, leaving a 15cm [6in] tail. Wrap the yarn around the knitting needle six times, taking care that your tension is similar to your knitting, and mark the spot you reach (I use a locking stitch marker or a pin).

1 Thread the yarn onto a sashiko needle (or a similar sharp needle with an eye large enough for your yarn).

2 Insert the needle into the centre of your yarn at the marked spot (the marker has been removed here to facilitate insertion), and continue through your yarn for approximately 4cm [1½in].

November

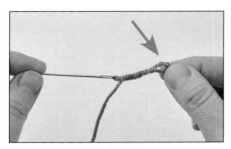

3 Pull the needle through to create a small loop, which is positioned at the marked spot.

4 Thread the end of your new yarn through the loop made in the old yarn.

5 Gently pull on your old yarn to tighten the small loop.

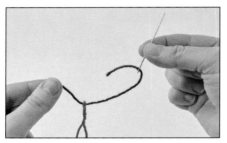

6 Thread the end of the new yarn onto the sashiko needle.

7 Pass the needle back through the centre of your yarn for approximately 4cm [1½in] to create an interlocking loop with the old yarn.

8 Pull the needle through.

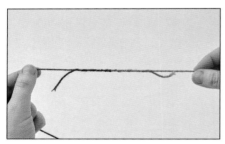

9 Gently pull on the two ends to tighten the join.

10 Trim the ends of each yarn.

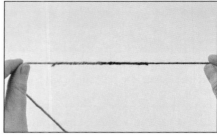

11 You now have two yarns joined almost invisibly, and you can continue to work the last six stitches in pattern. Your colour change should land in just the right place. If you miss by a little, you can adjust your next colour change accordingly.

I hope that knowing how to work a yarn over at the start of a row, as well as how to use that yarn over edging to join strips of knitting together will allow you to create complex-looking modular patterns. They are much easier than they look! Working Emily's Findhorn Wrap will give you lots of opportunities to hone your modular knitting skills.

PROJECT
FINDHORN WRAP

by
Emily K. Williams

Modularly knitted rectangles in stocking and garter stitch create a dynamic, textured wrap.

November

SIZE
One size only
Length: 199cm [78¼in]
Width: 46cm [18¼in]

YARN
Coop Knits Socks Yeah! 4ply (4ply / fingering weight; 75% superwash merino, 25% nylon; 212m per 50g skein)
Yarn A: Melanite (121); 2 x 50g skeins
Yarn B: Danburite (105); 2 x 50g skeins
Yarn C: Citrine (118); 1 x 50g skein
Yarn D: Almandine (117); 1 x 50g skein
Yarn E: Quartz (122); 1 x 50g skein

Approximate yardages
Yarns A & B: 424m [462yds] each
Yarns C–E: 212m [231yds] each

NEEDLES AND NOTIONS
1 pair 3.25mm [US 3] knitting needles, circular needles may also be used, or size needed to match tension
Waste yarn or stitch holders
Tapestry needle
Optional: sashiko needle (or other sharp needle) for working a Russian join

TENSION
21 sts and 46 rows to 10cm [4in] over garter stitch, relaxed after washing and blocking
21 sts and 42 rows to 10cm [4in] over stocking stitch, relaxed after washing and blocking

ABBREVIATIONS
A full list of abbreviations can be found on page 112.

SPECIAL TECHNIQUES
Photo tutorials for the following techniques can be found within this book:
Working a yarn over at the start of a row (page 78)
Picking up and knitting a yarn over (page 79)
Russian join (pages 79–80)

The following video tutorials can be found on our website at **www.acknitwear.co.uk/confident-knitting**
Modular joining using yarn overs (includes working a yarn over at the start of a row)
Russian join
Knitting in ends

PATTERN NOTES
This wrap is worked in four strips, with bold coloured stripes and alternating garter and stocking stitch sections. All the stitches are cast on and the border worked before putting stitches on hold and working the first strip. This first strip has a simple border on the right-hand edge, and yarn overs on the left-hand side. The second (and subsequent) strips are joined by picking up and knitting into these yarn overs as the knitting progresses. The wrap is completed with a small garter stitch border.

To achieve a clean colour change at the start of each stripe, a Russian join may be used. Alternatively, leave the ends loose at the colour changes and weave them in later, or knit the ends in as you go.

The wrap pattern is provided in one size, but it would be very straightforward to adjust the width by adding (or removing) a multiple of 24 sts to the cast-on edge. You will then need to adjust the number of strips worked. You can also adjust the length of the wrap, by working fewer (or extra) blocks in each strip.

WRAP

1 CAST ON AND WORK BORDER
Using yarn A, cast on 97 sts using the long-tail cast on, or your preferred cast-on method.

Row 1 (RS): Sl1 pwise wyif, knit to end.
Row 2 (WS): Sl1 pwise wyif, knit to end.
Rows 3–5: Work rows 1 and 2 once more, then work row 1 again.
Row 6: Sl1 pwise wyif, k1, *yo, k2tog; rep from * to last st, k1.

Change to yarn B.

2 WORK STRIPS
STRIP 1
With RS facing, arrange sts so that the first 25 sts of the row remain on the needles, and the remaining 72 sts are transferred to waste yarn or a holder. Work Strip 1 using the colours and blocks indicated in the table overleaf.

Cut yarn and place the 25 sts onto waste yarn or a holder.

STRIP 2
With RS facing, transfer the next 24 sts from the border holder to the working needles. Work using the colours and blocks indicated in the table overleaf.

Cut yarn and place the 24 sts onto waste yarn or a holder.

STRIP 3
With RS facing, transfer the next 24 sts from the border holder to the working needles. Work using the colours and blocks indicated in the table overleaf.

Cut yarn and place the 24 sts onto waste yarn or a holder.

STRIP 4
With RS facing, transfer the remaining 24 sts from the border holder to the working needles. Work using the colours and blocks indicated in the table overleaf.

When you have completed strip 4, cut yarn.

3 FINAL BORDER
Transfer the held sts from strips 1–3 to working needle. With RS facing join in yarn A. *97 sts.*
Rows 1–4: Sl1 pwise wyif, knit to end.

Cast off all sts, taking care to keep the edge loose.

4 FINISHING
Weave in any remaining ends, but do not trim. Soak wrap in lukewarm water and wool wash for 20 minutes, squeeze out excess water and press between towels to dry further. Lay flat to measurements and allow to dry. Once completely dry trim any remaining ends.

November

BLOCK INSTRUCTIONS

BLOCK 1
Row 1 (RS): Sl1 pwise wyif, k24. *25 sts.*
Row 2 (WS): Yo, k2tog, knit to last 3 sts, yo, k2tog, k1.
Row 3: Sl1 pwise wyif, knit to end.
Rows 4–23: Work rows 2–3 a further 10 times.
Row 24 (WS): *Yo, k2tog; rep from * to last st, k1.
Change yarn (see table for next shade).

BLOCK 2
Row 1 (RS): Sl1 pwise wyif, knit to end.
Row 2 (WS): Yo, p2tog, purl to last 3 sts, yo, k2tog, k1.
Row 3: Sl1 pwise wyif, knit to end.
Rows 4–23: Work rows 2–3 a further 10 times.
Row 24 (WS): *Yo, p2tog; rep from * to last 3 sts, yo, k2tog, k1.
Change yarn (see table for next shade).

BLOCK 3
Row 1 (RS): Pick up and knit the yo from the border row (next to the left needle tip and already joined to the previous strip), k2tog, k22. *24 sts.*
Row 2 (WS): Yo, p2tog, purl to end.
Row 3: Pick up and knit yo from previous strip, k2tog, knit to end.
Rows 4–23: Work rows 2–3 a further 10 times.
Row 24 (WS): *Yo, p2tog; rep from * to end.
Change yarn (see table for next shade).

BLOCK 4
Row 1 (RS): Pick up and knit the next yo (the last before a colour change), k2tog, knit to end.
Row 2 (WS): Yo, k2tog, knit to end.
Row 3: Pick up and knit yo from previous strip, k2tog, knit to end.
Rows 4–23: Work rows 2–3 a further 10 times.
Row 24 (WS): *Yo, k2tog; rep from * to end.
Change yarn (see table for next shade).

BLOCK 5
Row 1 (RS): Pick up and knit the next yo (the last before a colour change), k2tog, knit to end.
Row 2 (WS): Yo, p2tog, purl to end.
Row 3: Pick up and knit yo from previous strip, k2tog, knit to end.
Rows 4–23: Work rows 2–3 a further 10 times.
Row 24 (WS): *Yo, p2tog; rep from * to end.
Change yarn (see table for next shade).

BLOCK 6
Row 1 (RS): Pick up and knit the yo from the border row (next to the left needle tip and already joined to the previous strip), k2tog, k22. *24 sts.*
Row 2 (WS): Yo, k2tog, knit to end.
Row 3: Pick up and knit yo from previous strip, k2tog, knit to end.
Rows 4–23: Work rows 2–3 a further 10 times.
Row 24 (WS): *Yo, k2tog; rep from * to end.
Change yarn (see table for next shade).

BLOCK 7
Row 1 (RS): Pick up and knit the yo from the border row (next to the left needle tip and already joined to the previous strip), k2tog, k22. *24 sts.*
Row 2 (WS): Sl1 pwise wyif, k1, yo, p2tog, purl to end.
Row 3: Pick up and knit yo from previous strip, k2tog, knit to end.
Rows 4–23: Work rows 2–3 a further 10 times.
Row 24 (WS): Sl1 pwise wyif, k1, *yo, p2tog; rep from * to end.
Change yarn (see table for next shade).

BLOCK 8
Row 1 (RS): Pick up and knit the next yo (the last before a colour change), k2tog, knit to end.
Row 2 (WS): Sl1 pwise wyif, k1, yo, k2tog, knit to end.
Row 3: Pick up and knit yo from previous strip, k2tog, knit to end.
Row 4–23: Work rows 2–3 a further 10 times.
Row 24 (WS): Sl1 pwise wyif, k1, *yo, k2tog; rep from * to end.
Change yarn (see table for next shade).

BLOCK 9
Row 1 (RS): Pick up and knit the next yo (the last before a colour change), k2tog, knit to end.
Row 2 (WS): Sl1 pwise wyif, k1, yo, p2tog, purl to end.
Row 3: Pick up and knit yo from previous strip, k2tog, knit to end.
Rows 4–23: Work rows 2–3 a further 10 times.
Row 24 (WS): Sl1 pwise wyif, k1, *yo, p2tog; rep from * to end.
Change yarn (see table for next shade).

TABLE OF COLOURS AND BLOCKS

Read this as a table, starting at the top of Strip 1, and working
colours and blocks in numerical order, down the column.

Number	STRIP 1 Colour	STRIP 1 Block	STRIP 2 Colour	STRIP 2 Block	STRIP 3 Colour	STRIP 3 Block	STRIP 4 Colour	STRIP 4 Block
1	B	1	A	3	A	6	C	7
2	C	2	D	4	B	5	E	8
3	B	1	A	5	A	4	C	9
4	C	2	D	4	B	5	E	8
5	B	1	A	5	A	4	C	9
6	C	2	D	4	B	5	E	8
7	B	1	B	5	A	4	B	9
8	D	2	E	4	B	5	A	8
9	B	1	B	5	A	4	B	9
10	D	2	E	4	B	5	A	8
11	B	1	B	5	A	4	B	9
12	D	2	E	4	B	5	A	8
13	C	1	B	5	A	4	B	9
14	B	2	C	4	C	5	A	8
15	C	1	B	5	A	4	B	9
16	B	2	C	4	C	5	A	8
17	C	1	B	5	A	4	B	9
18	B	2	C	4	C	5	A	8
19	E	1	D	5	A	4	B	9
20	A	2	E	4	D	5	E	8
21	E	1	D	5	A	4	B	9
22	A	2	E	4	D	5	E	8
23	E	1	D	5	A	4	B	9
24	A	2	E	4	D	5	E	8
25	D	1	B	5	A	4	B	9
26	A	2	E	4	B	5	D	8
27	D	1	B	5	A	4	B	9
28	A	2	E	4	B	5	D	8
29	D	1	B	5	A	4	B	9
30	A	2	E	4	B	5	D	8
31	B	1	A	5	E	4	A	9
32	C	2	C	4	A	5	D	8
33	B	1	A	5	E	4	A	9
34	C	2	C	4	A	5	D	8
35	B	1	A	5	E	4	A	9
36	C	2	C	4	A	5	D	8

Winter

December
TECHNIQUE **Long-Tail and German Twisted Cast On For Ribbing**
PROJECT **Stellar Hat**
DESIGNER **Gudrun Johnston**

January
TECHNIQUE **Grab Stitches**
PROJECT **Saturnus Cushions**
DESIGNER **Jimenez Joseph**

February
TECHNIQUE **i-Cord Cast Off**
PROJECT **Prime Blanket**
DESIGNER **Carol Feller**

TECHNIQUE
LONG-TAIL AND GERMAN TWISTED CAST ON FOR RIBBING

Many of us have one go-to cast-on method that we use most of the time. It's completely normal to find a process that works well for you, and to stick with it! However, this month I'd like to make the case for trying something new...

The combination of the long-tail and German twisted cast on is a great option for ribbing. The long-tail cast-on method sets up the knit stitches perfectly, and the German twisted cast-on method sets up the purl stitches, but also adds an extra level of stretch to the edging. This is perfect for the brim of a hat, as in Gudrun Johnston's elegant Stellar Hat, but it's also fabulous for cuff-down socks, where the extra stretchiness of the German twisted method is particularly welcome.

If you already use the long-tail method for casting on, you'll find that this is just a small extra movement for a great benefit.

Note: To get a feel for how long of a long tail you need to leave for this cast-on method, wrap the yarn around your needle ten times. Pinch the ends and unwrap the yarn. Use this length to measure how much yarn is required for the number of stitches you need to cast on. For example, if you need to cast on 128 stitches, you will require 13 times the length you measured for ten stitches. Make your slip knot at the end of the tail you have measured out.

LONG-TAIL AND GERMAN TWISTED CAST-ON METHOD FOR RIBBING

1 Leaving a long tail (see note opposite), make a slip knot and place it on your needle so that the tail is on the left, towards you and the ball of yarn is on the right, away from you. This works as the first cast-on stitch.

2 Place your thumb and index finger of your left hand between the tail and working yarn hanging from the needle.

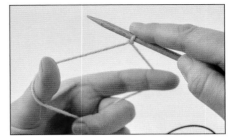

3 Grasp the tail and working yarn with your remaining fingers on your left hand. Your thumb and index finger are open with the yarn passing over them.

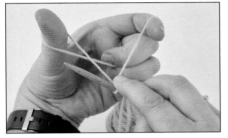

4 Bring the needle down, putting your right index finger on the slip knot to hold it in place, so that you create a Y-shape with the yarn and needle. If you hold the needle towards the thumb, it makes a loop with the yarn on the thumb.

5 Bring the needle tip up through the loop of yarn on your thumb, with the tip of the needle parallel with your thumb.

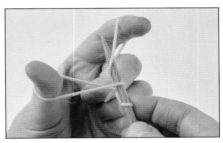

6 Now bring your needle tip over the top of the yarn on your index finger.

7 Pull the index finger yarn through the loop on your thumb.
8 Release the loop from your thumb

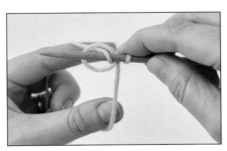

and gently tighten the yarn to form a stitch on your needle.

9 Steps 4–8 create a stitch with the long-tail cast-on method. For ribbing, we will use the long-tail cast-on stitches for the knit stitches.

December

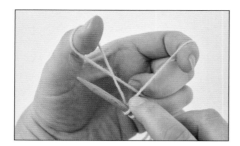

10 Return to the Y-shape with the needle towards your thumb, to create a loop of yarn around your thumb.

11 Instead of bringing the needle tip up inside the loop, bring it towards your body and pass under both strands of thumb loop yarn. coming back up between your thumb and index finger.

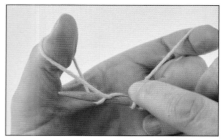

12 Bring the needle tip down into the loop of yarn on your thumb.

13 Bring the tip of the needle towards your body and then up and over the yarn on your index finger.

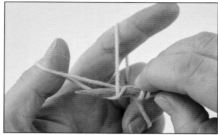

14 Use the needle tip to pull the index finger yarn through the loop on your thumb.

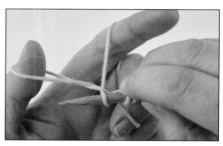

15 Because the loop of yarn on your thumb is twisted, you may need to wiggle your thumb to bring the index finger yarn fully through the loop.

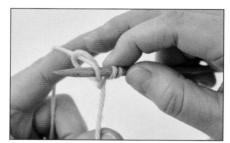

16 Release the loop of yarn from your thumb and gently tighten to form a stitch on your needle.

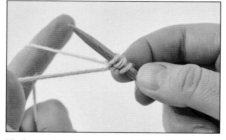

17 Steps 10–16 create a stitch with the German twisted cast-on method. For ribbing, we will use the German twisted cast-on stitches for the purl stitches.

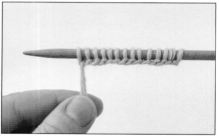

18 Continue to cast on a combination of long-tail and German twisted stitches as required by your ribbing pattern. Here the stitches are set up for knit 2, purl 2 rib, beginning and ending with knits.

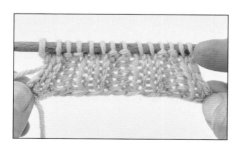

19 LEFT: Once you have worked some rib over your cast-on stitches, you will see that they form a pleasingly stretchy edge.
If you find that you need even more stretch in your cast-on edge, try spacing out the stitches more as you cast on. The loops of yarn at

the base of your cast-on stitches affect the length of the cast-on edge, rather than the needle size you use. Spacing out your stitches means that the loops at the base are larger, and your cast-on edge will be looser.

PROJECT
STELLAR HAT

by Gudrun Johnston

The combination of German twisted and long-tail cast ons provides the perfect amount of stretch for the brim of this beautiful hat.

December

SIZES

Small (Medium, Large, XL)

To fit head circumference: 45 (51, 57, 65) cm [17¾ (20, 22½, 25½) in]

Hat circumference at brim: 40 (45.5, 51.5, 57) cm [15¾, 18, 20¼, 22½) in]

Hat circumference at widest point: 44.5 (53.5, 62, 71) cm [17½ (21, 24½, 28) in]

Length from brim to crown (as worn): 24 (24.5, 25, 25.5) cm [9¼ (9½, 9¾, 10) in]

Shown in size Medium on head circumference 55cm [21½in].

YARN

Jamieson & Smith 2ply Jumper Weight (4ply weight/fingering; 100% Shetland wool; 115m per 25g ball)

Yarn A: Shade 21; 1 x 25g ball in all sizes

Yarn B: Shade 203; 2 (2, 3, 3) x 25g balls

Yarn C: Shade FC34; 1 x 25g ball in all sizes

Approximate yardages

Yarn A: 80 (90, 95, 105) m [85 (95, 105, 115) yds]

Yarn B: 165 (205, 245, 285) m [180 (220, 265, 310) yds]

Yarn C: 35 (45, 50, 60) m [40 (45, 55, 65) yds]

Yarn A includes approximately 45m [50yds] for a pompom.

NEEDLES AND NOTIONS

1 set 3mm [US 2] circular needles, 40cm [16in] long (for brim), or your preferred needles for working small circumferences

in the round, or size needed to match rib pattern tension

1 set 3.5mm [US 4] circular needles, 40cm [16in] long (for body of hat), or your preferred needles for working small circumferences in the round, or size needed to match stranded colourwork pattern tension

1 set 3.5mm [US 4] double-pointed needles (for crown shaping), or your preferred needles for working small circumferences in the round, or size needed to match stranded colourwork pattern tension

Stitch marker, Tapestry needle, Pompom maker (optional)

TENSION

27 sts and 32 rounds to 10cm [4in] over stranded colourwork pattern on larger needles, after washing and blocking

28 sts and 40 rounds to 10cm [4in] in 2x2 rib pattern on smaller needles, after washing and blocking

ABBREVIATIONS

k1-r/b   knit 1 into the row below; Turn the left needle slightly towards you so that you can see the wrong side of the work. Insert right needle from the top down into the purl stitch that sits below the first stitch on the left needle. Knit this stitch, then knit the stitch on the needle (1 stitch increased).

A full list of abbreviations can be found on page 112.

SPECIAL TECHNIQUES

Long-tail and German twisted cast on for ribbing (pages 89–90)

The following video tutorials can be found on our website at **www.acknitwear.co.uk/confident-knitting**

Long-tail and German twisted cast on for ribbing

Holding yarns for stranded colourwork

Joining in yarns

PATTERN NOTES

The hat starts with a contrast colour cast on, using a combination of the long-tail and German twisted cast-on methods, before a deep ribbed brim is worked. The piece is then turned inside out (so that the contrast edge sits correctly). The body of the hat is worked in a simple stranded colourwork pattern, followed by crown shaping. The hat can be topped with a pompom, or not, as you wish!

The pattern is provided in four sizes, but if you wish to make further adjustments, here are some suggestions. To alter the depth, knit the ribbed brim to a different length. If you wish to alter the depth of the chart A colourwork motif section, add or remove colourwork rounds from the start of the chart, so that you still end on chart row 7. The easiest way to alter the circumference is to use a smaller or larger needle or a different weight of yarn, but you will need to work a swatch to be sure you are getting a fabric that you like, and then calculate what size of hat you will make using your new tension information.

HAT

1 CAST ON AND WORK RIBBING

Using smaller needles and yarn A, cast on 112 (128, 144, 160) sts as follows (see also photo tutorial tutorial on pages 89–90):
Make a slip knot and place on needle as the first cast-on stitch.
Cast on 1 st using the long-tail method, then cast on 2 sts using the German twisted method, *cast on 2 sts using the long-tail method, then cast on 2 sts using the German twisted method; rep from * until 112 (128, 144, 160) sts have been cast on.
Join to work in the round, being careful not to twist. Pm for start of round.

Change to yarn B and knit 1 round.

Round 1: *K2, p2; rep from * to end.
Last round sets 2x2 rib pattern. Continue to work in rib pattern for a further 35 (39, 43, 47) rounds (36 (40, 44, 48) rounds in rib worked in total).

Push the knitting through the centre of the needles so that WS is now facing (yarn will be attached to the st on the left needle).
Bring yarn to front of work, slip first st purlwise, pull working yarn up and over needle ready to knit the next st (the st will look like it is a double st, as for a German short row).

Knit the next stitch and then continue in the rib pattern to end of round.
Next round: Insert the tip of the right needle (try to only use the tip) into the first leg of the double stitch, knit it and take it off the needle, then using tip of right needle only again, knit the second leg of the double stitch together with the next st on the needle. Continue in rib pattern to end of round.

CHART NOTES

The hat is worked in the round, so all chart rows are read from right to left.

2 MAIN HAT BODY

Small only
Inc round: *[K2, p2] 3 times, k1-r/b, k1, p2, [k2, p2] twice, k1-r/b, k1, p2; rep from * to end. *8 sts inc; 120 sts.*

Medium only
Inc round: *K2, p2, k1-r/b, k1, p2; rep from * to end. *16 sts inc; 144 sts.*

Large only
Inc round: *K2, p2, [k1-r/b, k1, p2] twice; rep from * to end. *24 sts inc; 168 sts.*

XL only
Inc round: *K2, p2, [k1-r/b, k1, p2] 4 times; rep from * to end. *32 sts inc; 192 sts.*

CHART B: Crown shaping

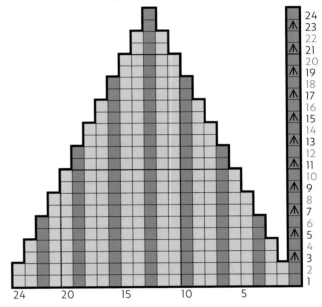

KEY

■ (dark)	Using yarn A (21); knit
□ (light)	Using yarn B (203); knit
■ (grey)	Using yarn C (FC34); knit
⋀	Using shade indicated; sl 2 as if to k2tog, k1, pass 2 slipped stitches over
2, 4, 6, etc...	For rounds indicated in pink, do not work final stitch of round; slip this last stitch to right needle, remove marker, return slipped stitch to left needle, replace marker.

CHART A: Body

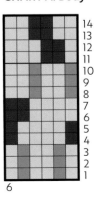

December

All sizes
Change to larger needles and knit 1 round in yarn B.

Round 1: Work across 6 sts from row 1 of chart A 20 (24, 28, 32) times.
Last round sets chart A pattern. Continue to work from chart A, changing yarns as indicated, until chart row 14 is complete. Work rows 1-14 of chart A once more and then work rows 1-7 once more.

3 CROWN SHAPING
Note: *During the crown shaping chart 10 (12, 14, 16) sts are decreased on every decrease round. It is necessary to stop 1 stitch before the beginning of each decrease round and then slip this last stitch to right needle, remove marker, return slipped stitch to left needle, replace marker and then begin decrease round.*

As crown gets smaller, switch to DPNs (or your preferred needles for working small circumferences in the round) when required, to work comfortably around hat.

Round 1: Work across 24 sts from row 1 of chart B 5 (6, 7, 8) times.
Last round sets chart B pattern. Continue to work from chart B, decreasing as indicated (see previous note), until chart row 24 is complete. *110 (132, 154, 176) sts dec; 10 (12, 14, 16) sts remain.*

Break yarn and thread through remaining sts.

4 FINISHING
Weave in all ends. Soak your hat in lukewarm water with wool wash for 20 minutes. Squeeze out the excess water. Lay flat to dry, taking care not to overstretch the ribbing, or dry over a hat form or balloon or stuff with plastic bags. Leave to dry. If desired, make a pompom and attach firmly to the crown of the hat.

TECHNIQUE
GRAB STITCHES

Grab stitches are an extraordinarily fun way to add texture to your knitting. The basic method for working grab stitches is very straightforward: you pick up a purl bump from a few rows below your next stitch, and that bump is then worked with the next stitch. The versatility of grab stitches comes from the many ways in which they can be used.

Grab stitches are worked on the purl side of the fabric, but the finished fabric can use either the purl or knit side as the right side. Grab stitches can also be worked singly, which gives a "stretched stitch" appearance, or they can be worked in groups, which creates a more 3D, folded effect in your finished fabric.

Jimenez Joseph's tactile Saturnus Cushions showcase all of these possibilities. The orange version uses a single grab stitch with the purl side of the fabric as right side. This gives a finished effect reminiscent of dip stitches, with strands of yarn lying over the fabric. The blue-grey Saturnus Cushion is knitted with a series of grab stitches worked together, and the knit side of the fabric on display. Using multiple grab stitches together creates sculptural folds in the fabric, evoking ripples or waves.

GRAB STITCH TERMINOLOGY
Stitch patterns are referred to as grab stitch 1x4, where the first number is how many stitches are grabbed and the second number is how many rows down you grab them.

So the orange Saturnus Cushion uses a grab stitch 1x4 pattern, where one grab stitch is worked four rows down in each section.

The blue-grey Saturnus Cushion uses a grab stitch 4x6 pattern. In this pattern four grab stitches are worked, one after the other, and each one picks up a purl bump six rows down.

Single grab stitches with the purl side as RS.

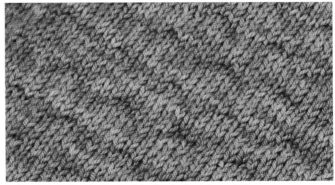

Single grab stitches with the knit side as RS.

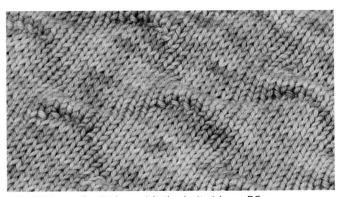

Multiple grab stitches with the knit side as RS.

Multiple grab stitches with the purl side as RS.

January

GRAB STITCH 1x4

1 Work as directed to the first grab stitch instruction.

2 Count down four purl bumps below the next stitch on the left needle. The right needle tip is pointing at the fourth bump.

3 Using your right needle tip, pick up that bump from bottom to top.

4 Insert your right needle tip knitwise into the next stitch on your left needle.

5 Slip the stitch to your right needle.

6 Insert your left needle tip into both the picked-up bump and the slipped stitch on the right needle, from right to left, and slip them to your left needle.

7 This reorients the stitches correctly.

8 Now purl these two stitches together.

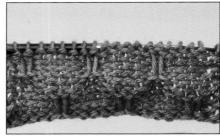

9 Once the row is complete, you will have a series of elongated stitches stretched across the purl side of the fabric.

GRAB STITCH 4x6

1 Work as directed to the first grab stitch instruction.

2 Count down six purl bumps below the next stitch on your left needle. The right needle tip is pointing at the sixth bump.

3 Using your right needle tip, pick up that bump from bottom to top.

4 Insert your right needle tip knitwise into the next stitch on your left needle and slip that stitch to your right needle.

5 Insert your left needle tip into both the picked-up bump and the slipped stitch on the right needle, from right to left, and slip them to your left needle.

6 This reorients the stitches correctly.

7 Now purl these two stitches together.

8 That completes your first Grab stitch 4x6. The first grab stitch will appear elongated, but once you have worked a few more, the fabric will fold and the elongation will disappear.

9 Repeat steps 2–7 a further three times.

10 From the knit side of the fabric you can see the folded texture more clearly.

I hope you're feeling confident to add lots of grab stitch texture to your upcoming projects. With two different options, Jimenez's Saturnus Cushions will get you grabbing stitches like a professional.

PROJECT
SATURNUS CUSHIONS

by Jimenez Joseph

Grab stitches create two options for gloriously textured cushions.

SIZES
One size only
To fit a cushion: 40cm x 40cm [16in x 16in]
Actual cushion cover width (takes account of seaming): 38cm [15in]
Actual cushion cover height (including rib): 42cm [16½in]

YARN
Third Vault Yarns Caroline DK (DK weight; 100% superwash merino; 230m per 115g skein)
Saturnus; 2 x 115g skeins for the orange grab stitch 1x4 cushion
Enceladus; 2 x 115g skeins for the blue-grey grab stitch 4x6 cushion
Approximate yardage per cushion
455m [495yds]

NEEDLES AND NOTIONS
One pair 5mm [US 8] knitting needles, or size needed to match grab stitch tension
One pair 3.5mm [US 4] knitting needles, or size needed to match rib tension
Tapestry needle
Six 20mm [¾in] buttons
One cushion pad 40cm x 40cm [16in x 16in]
Crochet hook approximately 3.5mm (optional)

TENSION
20 sts and 30 rows to 10cm [4in] over either grab stitch pattern using larger needles, after washing and blocking
22 sts and 36 rows to 10cm [4in] over 2x2 rib pattern using smaller needles, after washing and blocking

ABBREVIATIONS
Grab stitch 1x4 See photo tutorial on page 96. Using your right needle tip, pick up the purl bump 4 stitches below the next stitch on your left needle from bottom to top. Slip the next stitch on the left needle knitwise. Insert the left needle into the grabbed stitch and slipped stitches on your right needle (in that order). This returns them to the left needle in the correct position. Purl the grabbed and slipped stitches together.

Grab stitch 4x6 See photo tutorial on page 97. Using your right needle tip, pick up the purl bump 6 stitches below the next stitch on your left needle from bottom to top. Slip the next stitch on the left needle knitwise. Insert the left needle into the grabbed stitch and slipped stitches on your right needle (in that order). This returns them to the left needle in the correct position. Purl the grabbed and slipped stitches together. Repeat this process a further 3 times.

A full list of abbreviations can be found on page 112.

SPECIAL TECHNIQUES
Photo tutorials for the following techniques can be found within this book:
Grab stitches (page 96–97)

The following video tutorials can be found on our website at **www.acknitwear.co.uk/confident-knitting**
Grab stitches
Mattress stitch for stocking stitch
Mattress stitch for reverse stocking stitch

PATTERN NOTES
The Saturnus Cushion covers are cast on at the button band. By using the working yarn, rather than a provisional waste yarn, for the crochet cast on, the cast-on edge matches the cast-off edge perfectly. The body of the cushion is worked back and forth in your chosen grab stitch pattern, before ending with a buttonhole band. The cover is then seamed with mattress stitch and buttons are sewn on to the button band. Fill your cushion cover with a cushion pad and enjoy your work!

This pattern is provided in one size only, but the pattern is versatile if you wish to make a different size. You could adjust the width of your cushion cover by changing the number of cast-on stitches. For the grab stitch 1x4 pattern you will need to adjust by a multiple of six stitches, and for the grab stitch 4x6 pattern you will need to adjust by a multiple of 16 stitches. For small changes in size, stitches in stocking stitch or reverse stocking stitch can be added or removed at the sides. To change the height of your cover, change the number of repeats of the stitch pattern worked before the buttonhole band.

CHART NOTES
The cushion covers are worked flat, so odd-numbered RS chart rows are read from right to left. Even-numbered WS chart rows are read from left to right.

January

CUSHION

1 CAST ON AND MAKE BUTTON BAND

Using your main yarn (instead of waste yarn) and smaller knitting needles, work steps 1–5 of the crochet provisional cast-on method (page 9), then repeat steps 2–4 until you have 77 sts on your knitting needle. Slip the stitch from your crochet hook onto the knitting needle to create the final stitch. *78 sts.*

Row 1 (RS): *K2, p2; rep from * to last 2 sts, k2.
Row 2 (WS): P2, *k2, p2; rep from * to end.
Last 2 rows set 2x2 rib pattern. Work a further 10 rows in 2x2 rib (12 rows of 2x2 rib).

For grab stitch 1x4 move to step 2 and for grab stitch 4x6 move to step 3.

2 MAIN BODY – GRAB STITCH 1x4

Change to larger needles.

The following stitch pattern is also shown in chart A.
Row 1 (RS): Purl.
Row 2 (WS): Knit.
Rows 3–4: Work rows 1–2 once more.
Row 5: P3, *p4, work grab stitch 1x4, p1; rep from * to last 3 sts, p3.
Row 6: Knit.
Rows 7–10: Work rows 1–2 twice more.
Row 11: P3, *p1, work grab stitch 1x4, p4; rep from * to last 3 sts, p3.
Row 12: Knit.
Rows 1–12 set grab stitch 1x4 pattern. Continue to work in pattern until row 6 is completed for the 20th time (234 pattern rows worked).

Move to step 4.

3 MAIN BODY – GRAB STITCH 4x6

Change to larger needles.

The following stitch pattern is also shown in chart B.
Row 1 (RS): Knit.
Row 2 (WS): Purl.
Rows 3–9: Work rows 1–2 a further 3 times, then work row 1 once more.
Row 10: P7, *p2, work grab stitch 4x6, p10; rep from * to last 7 sts, p7.
Rows 11–19: Work rows 1–2 a further 4 times, then work row 1 once more.
Row 20: P7, *p10, work grab stitch 4x6, p2; rep from * to last 7 sts, p7.
Rows 1–20 set grab stitch 4x6 pattern. Continue to work in pattern until row 14 is complete for the 12th time (234 pattern rows worked).

Move to step 4.

KEY

☐	Knit on RS, purl on WS
⊡	Purl on RS, knit on WS
▦	Purl on WS, this is the stitch that is grabbed
⊡	Purl on RS, this is the stitch that is grabbed
↓	Grab stitch (see photo tutorial)
☐	Pattern repeat

CHART A: Grab stitch 1x4

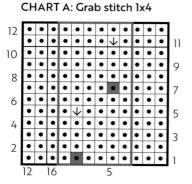

CHART B: Grab stitch 4x6

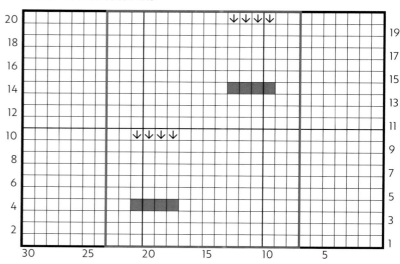

4 WORK BUTTONHOLE BAND AND CAST OFF
Change to smaller needles.

Row 1 (RS): *K2, p2; rep from * to last 2 sts, k2.
Row 2 (WS): P2, *k2, p2; rep from * to end.
Rows 3–6: Work rows 1–2 twice more.
Row 7: [K2, p2] twice, *k2tog, [yo] twice, rib 10 sts as set; rep from * to last 10 sts, k2tog, [yo] twice, [p2, k2] twice.
Row 8: Work in rib as set, dropping the second yo for each buttonhole.
Rows 9–12: Work rows 1–2 twice more.

Cast off all sts in pattern.

5 FINISHING
Fold the cushion cover so that both ribbed bands are lined up, with WS innermost and RS facing outwards. Thread a tapestry needle with a length of main yarn approximately 70cm [27½in] in length. Using the mattress stitch technique and taking in 1 stitch from each edge, starting from the ribbing end, sew the sides together, down to the folded corner. Repeat for the other side.

Sew buttons in position on the inside of the button band, directly opposite each buttonhole. Weave in ends.

Soak your cushion cover in lukewarm water with wool wash for 20 minutes. Squeeze out excess water. Lay flat to measurements and allow to dry.

TECHNIQUE
I-CORD CAST OFF

Few techniques give a project a more professional finish than an i-cord cast off. An i-cord is a small tube of knitted stitches. These can be created using a knitting doll, knitting Nancy or French knitting tool, or can be knitted on straight needles as described below. The term i-cord was first coined by Elizabeth Zimmermann and the "i" stands for idiot. She describes it in *Knitting Without Tears* as, "Idiot's Delight: an easy knitted cord". Small knitted tubes had been known for a long time, but Zimmermann developed many applications of this handy tube, including the i-cord cast off and cast on, i-cord buttonholes and many more clever innovations.

Carol Feller's snuggly Prime Blanket uses the i-cord cast off to add a level of elegance and polish to this simple design. The hidden pocket is finished with an i-cord edging, as are the edges of the blanket itself. Although it is possible to start a project with an i-cord cast on, I find that starting with a standard or provisional cast on, and later working an i-cord cast off gives a neater finish. If you use a standard cast-on method, you will later need to pick up stitches along that edge.

PICKING UP STITCHES

In order to work an i-cord cast off around all of the edges of the Prime Blanket, stitches must be picked up along the row-end and cast-on edges. The following tutorial will show you how to do this.

1 Work your final right side row and place a marker after the last stitch. This marker will denote the corner.

2 Use your left needle to pick up the stitch at the very edge of the fabric, under the final stitch on your right needle.

3 Knit both loops of the picked-up stitch together.

4 Use your left needle to pick up the stitch in the next row down the edge of the blanket.

5 Knit both loops of the picked-up stitch together.

6 Repeat steps 4–5 once more. You have now picked up and knitted three stitches into three rows at the edge of the blanket.

7 Now miss out the next row, and pick up the stitch two rows down the edge of the blanket.

8 Knit both loops of the picked-up stitch together.

9 Continue in this way to pick up and knit three stitches in every four rows along the edge of the blanket, until you reach the cast-on edge.

10 Insert your needle tip into the first cast-on stitch, and knit into it.

11 Continue to work along the cast-on edge, knitting into every stitch.

February

12 Place a marker at the end of the cast-on edge to denote the corner.

13 Pick up and knit three stitches in every four rows along the second row-end edge of the blanket, following steps 2–9.

You now have live stitches on all four sides of your blanket. At each corner there is either a marker, or a join between two needles.

CABLE CAST-ON METHOD

Having picked-up stitches around the outside of the blanket, the next step is to cast on three stitches to be used as the i-cord stitches. The cable cast-on method is generally used.

1 Insert your right needle tip between the first and second stitches on the left needle, and wrap the yarn around the right needle tip.

2 Pull through a loop of yarn with your right needle tip.

3 Place that loop onto the left needle tip without twisting it. You have cast on one stitch with the cable method.

4 Repeat steps 1–3 twice more, so that you have cast on a total of three stitches. These are your i-cord stitches.

I-CORD CAST-OFF METHOD

Throughout the following instructions, the i-cord stitches will be worked, and joined to the picked-up stitches around the outside of the blanket. This will give an attractive cord-like appearance. Unjoined i-cord rows are also worked to ease the edging around the corners.

1 Knit the first two stitches on your left needle.

2 Slip the next stitch on your left needle, knitwise to your right needle.

3 Slip the next stitch on your left needle, purlwise (or knitwise) to your right needle.

4 Insert the left needle tip into the front of the two slipped stitches on your right needle tip, from left to right.

5 Knit the two slipped stitches together through the back loops.

6 Steps 2–5 create an ssk stitch that joins one i-cord stitch to one of the edging stitches of your blanket.

7 Slip all three stitches from your right needle to your left needle, without twisting them.

8 Repeat steps 1–7 until you reach your corner marker, omitting step 7 on the final repeat. Remove the marker.

9 Slip all three stitches from your right needle to your left needle, without twisting them.

10 Knit three stitches.

11 Repeat steps 9–10 once more.

12 Working two rounds of standard i-cord (steps 9–11), without joining to the blanket stitches, eases the edging around the corner. Continue to work steps 1–7 until your next corner marker.

You really can't beat an i-cord cast off for a smart way to complete a project. I hope you will enjoy trying it out on Carol Feller's lovely Prime Blanket.

PROJECT
PRIME BLANKET

by Carol Feller

With pocket detail and streamlined i-cord trim, this basketweave blanket is one-of-a-kind.

SIZES
Small (Medium, Large)
Depth: 88 (93, 120) cm [34¾ (36½, 47¼) in]
Width: 68 (87, 106) cm [26¾ (34¼, 41¾) in]

YARN
Stolen Stitches Nua Sport (sport weight; 60% merino wool, 20% yak, 20% linen; 140m per 50g skein)
Kitten Fluff (9810); 6 (8, 13) x 50g skeins
Shown in size Medium.

Approximate yardages
825 (1115, 1750) m [900 (1215, 1910) yds]

NEEDLES AND NOTIONS
2 sets of 3.75mm [US 5] circular needles, 100cm [40in] long, or size needed to match tension

Stitch markers
Tapestry needle
Waste yarn (a smooth cotton in a similar weight to the main yarn is preferable)

TENSION
21 sts and 32 rows to 10cm [4in] over basketweave stitch pattern, after washing and blocking

ABBREVIATIONS
A full list of abbreviations can be found on page 112.

SPECIAL TECHNIQUES
Photo tutorials for the following techniques can be found within this book:
Picking up stitches (page 103)
i-Cord cast-off method (pages 104–105)

The following video tutorials can be found on our website at
www.acknitwear.co.uk/confident-knitting
Picking up stitches
i-Cord Cast Off

PATTERN NOTES
The blanket is cast on and worked in basketweave pattern, before waste yarn stitches are used to mark the position for an afterthought pocket. The blanket body is then completed in basketweave pattern. Next, stitches are picked up around the remaining three blanket edges, before being cast off with the i-cord method. Finally, the pocket stitches are picked up from the edges of the waste yarn stitches. The pocket edge is worked with an i-cord cast off, and a pocket lining is knitted down from the remaining stitches, before being sewn into place.

It can help to place a stitch marker after each 8-stitch pattern repeat to keep track of your work.

BLANKET

1 CAST ON AND WORK BLANKET BODY
Cast on 143 (183, 223) sts using your preferred cast-on method.

The following basketweave stitch pattern is also shown in the chart below.

Row 1 (RS): Knit.
Row 2 (WS): P1, k5, *p3, k5; rep from * to last st, p1.
Row 3: K1, *p5, k3; rep from * to last 6 sts, p5, k1.
Row 4: As row 2.
Row 5: As row 1.
Row 6: P1, k1, *p3, k5; rep from * to last 5 sts, p3, k1, p1.
Row 7: K1, p1, k3, *p5, k3; rep from * to last 2 sts, p1, k1.
Row 8: As row 6.
Rows 1–8 set basketweave pattern. Work in basketweave pattern until piece measures approximately 78 (83, 100) cm [30¾ (32¾, 39¼) in] from cast-on edge, ending with a WS row.

2 POCKET
Next row (RS): Work in pattern to last 54 sts, using waste yarn k24, slip last 24 sts just worked back to left needle, work in patt to end of row with main yarn.

You now have 24 sts of waste yarn in your fabric. After completion of the blanket you will return to these sts, unpick the waste yarn and work an afterthought pocket.

Continue to work in basketweave pattern, until piece measures approximately 88 (93, 120) cm [34¾ (36½, 47¼) in] from cast-on edge, ending with a RS row.

KEY

☐ Knit on RS, purl on WS

⊡ Purl on RS, knit on WS

☐ Pattern repeat

CHART

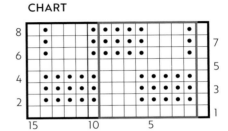

3 EDGING

Stitches will now be picked up and knitted around the remaining 3 sides of the knitted rectangle. See photo tutorial on page 103.

Pm, working down row-end edges of the blanket, pick up and knit 3 sts for every 4 rows to the corner, pm, with second long circular needle, working across cast-on sts, pick up and knit one st for every cast-on st, pm, working up row-end edge of the blanket, pick up and knit 3 sts for every 4 rows. Pm for start of round.
You will now have sts picked up all around the blanket on 2 needles with markers for each corner (if a marker falls at the end of your needle it can be omitted – just imagine there is a marker there!).

An i-cord cast off will now be worked around the blanket edges. See photo tutorials on pages 104–105.

Using the cable cast-on method, cast on 3 sts to left needle tip.

*[K2, ssk, slip all 3 stitches back to left needle] to marker, remove marker, [k3, slip all 3 sts back to left needle] twice; rep from * a further 3 times. *3 sts remain.*

K3tog, break yarn and draw yarn through final stitch.

4 POCKET

Using a spare needle, pick up the right leg (or side) of the 24 main yarn sts under the row of waste yarn stitches. Turn the blanket through 180° and use a second spare needle to pick up the main yarn stitches on the other side of the waste yarn. Carefully remove the waste yarn, ensuring all sts are safely on your needles.

Join yarn to the set of 24 sts closest to the cast-on edge of the blanket and work an i-cord cast off as follows:

Using the cable cast-on method, cast on 3 sts to left needle tip, adjacent to the 24 pocket sts.
*K2, ssk, slip all 3 sts back to left needle; rep from * until all of the lower pocket sts have been consumed. *3 sts remain.*
K3tog, break yarn and draw yarn through final stitch.

Join yarn to remaining 24 sts, with RS of work facing.
Row 1 (RS): Knit.
Row 2 (WS): Purl.
Continue to work in stocking stitch as set, until back of pocket measures 12cm [4¾in]. Cast off all sts.

5 FINISHING

Join start and end of i-cord edging together.

Using whip stitch, sew down sides of pocket carefully.

Weave in all ends, but do not trim.
Soak your blanket in lukewarm water and wool wash for 20 minutes. Squeeze out excess water (but do not wring). Press between towels to dry further. Lay your blanket flat to dry. When blanket is completely dry, trim any remaining ends.